Abuse is Not My Story

A message of hope through the destruction
of the power of abuse

Written by Victoria Elise Michael

Illustrated by Samantha Gustafson

ISBN 978-0-9983601-3-3

Scripture quotations marked (NIV) are taken from the Holy Bible, New International Version®, NIV®. Copyright ©1973, 1978, 1984, 2011 by Biblica, Inc.™ Used by permission of Zonderman. All rights reserved worldwide. www.zondervan.com The "NIV" and "New International Version" are trademarks registered in the United States Patent and Trademark Office by Biblica, Inc.™

Cover design and illustrations by Samantha Gustafson

Book layout design by Svetlana Kotova

Edited by Karen Engle

Cover photograph by Anita Charlton/Shutterstock.com

For Worldwide Distribution, Printed in the United States of America.

To protect the privacy of some of the individuals referred to, names, places, and other details have been changed.

Author's Note: This publication is designed to share a personal journey to freedom from abuse. It is sold with the understanding that the author is not engaged in rendering psychological, financial, legal, or other professional services. If expert assistance or counseling is needed, the services of a competent professional should be sought.

www.AbuseisNOTmystory.com

Dedication

I recently bought a vision board for my office at work. For me, a vision board is nothing more than a fancy corkboard, which contains pictures that represent my dreams, my vision. Finding this board was fun. I searched an online garage sale website. On this site, I found the perfect board – used, cheap, ignored, and identified by its owner based on the country-style frame surrounding it. With much excitement, I purchased this board for only $15. I bought the board because I believed it to be full of potential. This board would hold my visions. I was confident that the wood frame could adapt to any environment with only a small coat of paint. The board was unique, fun, and a perfect solution for my project.

This book is dedicated to many who have seen something unique, fun, promising, and special about me. Sometimes life is about shifting lenses to look at things from a different angle. Sometimes it is about recognizing that the core is special.

My journey has been just that. I have shifted my angle to live inside of the choices I make. I have recognized that my core is special.

I can't thank everyone who has believed in me. There are many, and I am grateful for each one of you. But I do want to acknowledge four people.

Charlotte is my counselor, my friend, my cheerleader, my investor, and just about any other positive adjective you can imagine. I told Charlotte that this book feels like a long thank-you note. It would be impossible to describe her investment in a couple of paragraphs, but you will read about it throughout the book. You will experience nuggets of her wisdom and investment as you are challenged to grow. Thank you, Charlotte, for helping to change my life and believing in me.

Carolyn is my long-term mentor, friend, spiritual encourager, and much more. You will hear a piece of her story – her choice to invest in me – in the investor chapter. Learning from and living life with Carolyn has been a blessing beyond my wildest expectations.

Finally, I have to tell you about the loves of my life: David and Lizzy. I could not dream of two more special children. They love freely. They live loudly. They care uniquely. And they share without limits. They are everything a mom could ask for in children. They are gifts from a loving God.

You will read about many people in this book who have cared deeply about me. I care deeply about them. Some individuals did not even make the book, but I still sincerely love them. As I share pieces of my story, things I've learned, and my struggles, I am also sharing pieces of myself, my friends and my God. It is a small way for me to extend to you the love that has been shown to me. Enjoy!

Table of Contents

Introduction

This book is a very personal journey, yet a journey common to many abuse survivors. It is the journey of finding yourself. It is the journey of determining what your story – your life – is about. This is the journey of healing. It is the journey of power. It is the journey of finding and experiencing freedom.

My hope is that your will join me on this journey. Healing is often hard, but it is always worth the effort. As we pursue understanding ourselves and freeing ourselves from a past defined by decisions someone else made to harm us, we will grow. We will learn to dream, to hope, to embrace the person who we were meant to be.

The book walks through five significant milestones. Milestone one is grabbing hold of hope beyond your experience. In chapters 1 and 2, we will give ourselves freedom to no longer be defined by choices that were made for us. We will intentionally focus our thoughts on the choices we have made. We will celebrate that we have the ability to become who we were created to be. At milestone two we will intentionally work toward creating the partnerships that will support us on the healing journey. We will explore the intricacies of friendships, as well as mentoring and counseling relationships that work. We will understand why these interactions are important and encouraging on our path to healing. At milestone three, we will work to create an atmosphere that facilitates growth. We will experience the freedom to celebrate small changes occurring in our lives. We will recognize that change often begins in a person's heart, not in their actions, and we will set boundaries that promote healthy growing environments. At milestone four, we will seek to understand our purpose. We are loved and loveable. We are special and unique. Our journey will ask us to consider the love relationship we have with our Heavenly Father. We will acknowledge anger, hurt, guilt and sorrow. We will be truthful and ask for healing. At the final milestone, milestone five, we will evaluate our own story. We will dream about our future. We will relax in being ourselves. We will learn that growth is rewarding and a lifelong journey.

I hope you will join me on this journey, and that it will bring you as much freedom as it has brought to me. Healing is what my heart desired. I needed help removing the obstacles blocking my view of what healing could look like. My goal in writing this book was to be real. I have struggled. I have fought. I have won. Today, my story is found. It is defined by the choices I am making to live my life today–a life of freedom, and acceptance that I am unique. I am different and special. I am not bound by my past.

Finally, this book is intended to challenge you. Each chapter will ask you to consider something new. Most chapters challenge you to engage in an exercise to embrace the concept of the chapter. Journal pages follow each chapter designed to help you evaluate, for yourself the importance of the concept presented in the chapter. I encourage you to be deeply personal. This is your journey. This is your chance to heal. Invest your energy into really evaluating what the chapter means for you.

Expert Considerations

Charlotte Cone received her bachelor's and masters from the University of Central Arkansas and her Ed.D. from the University of Memphis. Her degrees are in English, Counseling Services, and Higher Education Administration. As an educator, she spent 34 years in higher education at two- and four-year institutions. For the past 14 years she has had a private counseling practice and continues to see clients on part-time basis with plans to retire in 2018.

A MESSAGE FROM CHARLOTTE:

The author of this book is someone I have counseled for several years. She is a survivor. In her story, I think you will see a woman who knows she is confident, strong, intelligent, and hardworking; she is a woman who genuinely likes herself.

But more than that, she will share with you the big obstacles that an abused person faces – both internal and external challenges. She decided to make this book a guided journal so that you can experience some of the techniques she and others have used to overcome abuse. If you are looking for a nice cookbook approach or a magic answer to abuse, this book will not help you. If you want to understand abuse from a personal perspective and learn ways to help yourself and others, I think you will find this approach helpful and insightful.

Abuse is a difficult topic to talk about, whether you are the victim or know someone who has experienced it. If this book does one thing, it will give you hope. There is a way out of abuse.

Milestone 1:

Hope Beyond Your Experience

Chapter One: Abuse is Not My Story

I have wanted to write my story for years. In the depth of my heart I longed to write a story that would allow survivors to feel hope. But that was not my experience. My experience was dark. It felt like it had no end. At times, there was no hope, but instead, a daily fight to survive.

I still haven't found the end of my story, but I did find the beginning. And, when I found the beginning, I found light. I found hope. I finally found out that I could be alive, and not just survive.

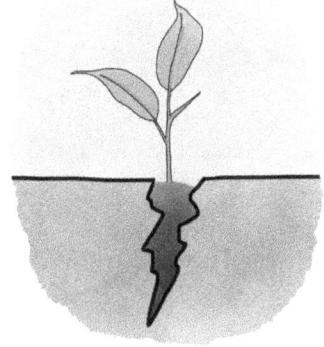

Let's start directly with where it began. I found hope when I finally understood these three truths:

1. Abuse is not "my story."
2. "My story" is created by the decisions I make.
3. I did not make the decision to be abused.

Yes, these concepts may seem basic. But if allowed to sink in, they will change your life. I am going to break each of them down. I want to challenge you. I want to encourage you to believe them.

But I have to be honest. I don't have a magic wand. I didn't believe these statements the first time I heard them. It is possible I didn't believe them the 100th time I heard them. But one day I did; today I still do. The journey is long, and healing forces you to face hurt that might overwhelm you. But you do have hope. You do have a future. You can be saved. Life can begin.

A few days after this three-line revelation hit me, an analogy sank deep in my soul. This analogy is a picture of what happened to me, and I'd love to share it with you. I had been living my life hidden below a concrete

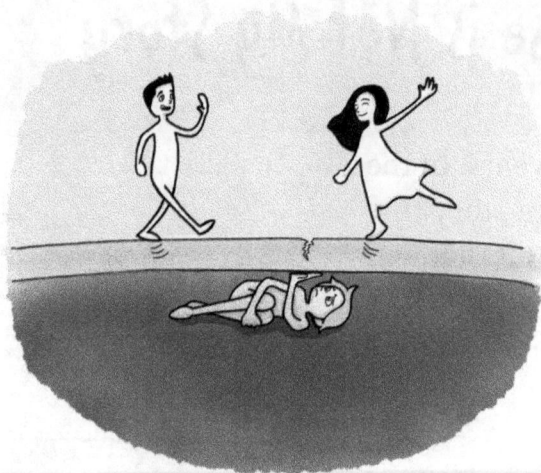

foundation of a house. Dirt and decay surrounded me, pressing in on my body from all sides. Above me was a concrete slab. Above the concrete slab I believed people lived life. I could hear footsteps of real life. Sometimes people were running because they were busy. Sometimes they were dancing because they were happy. And sometimes they were stomping in anger. But, they were living. I was not.

At times I would attempt to push away the dirt engulfing me. I wanted to move like the people above me did. But the dirt made no footsteps noises. Other times I would lie down and give up completely. I would accept that decay was inevitable. I would bury myself in dirt, inviting the decay to come sooner.

Finally, after the concrete slab grew old, the smallest crack formed. And now my belief that life occurred on top of the slab was confirmed. I couldn't understand it from my small view through the crack, but I knew it was happening. I needed a bigger crack. I fought for years and years to make the crack bigger. Finally, someone noticed I existed below the crack. They tried to help me out but couldn't. So they became a cheerleader. I had to destroy the concrete slab myself.

Cheerleaders came. At first it was one, then two, then ten, then more. And, another type of person came too – an investor. The investors dropped seeds in the crack. They said the seeds could grow and cause the crack to expand. The seeds gave me hope. The seeds healed parts of my decaying soul. Sometimes I quit fighting. The job was too big. Other times I fought hard. I accepted as many seeds as I could. The journey was long; the concrete was restricting and heavy. And the light I saw through the crack was almost invisible. But, over time, the concrete began to crack in more and more places. I began to see the life that existed above the dirt. I wanted it, and it terrified me at the same time. But, I kept fighting. Finally, a power drill came to attack the concrete. It was time for me to have the choice to leave the dirt. The power drill came because I finally understood. The drill was powered by a revelation deep in my soul – a revelation that I did not choose to be born in the dirt, and that my choices were my story. It was a revelation that if I wanted to live my story above the concrete slab, I could.

I had invested in good choices for years. I had fought to break the concrete. The cracks were because I knew I was worth more than dirt and decay. I had accepted the healing seeds. I had made cracks that gave them light to grow. My story was created by the decisions I made. I did not make the decision that forced me to fight the concrete. And with a deep breath and a loud yell, I released from deep inside of me a power that erupted through the cracks, fueled the power drill, and destroyed the concrete slab.

For the first time light appeared. It was beautiful, and it felt so amazing in my soul. As I moved, dirt fell off of me. It was no longer attached. It was no longer painfully pressed into me. I shook it off with a furry. The dirt was not my decision. I had a new life and my life, my story, was created by the decisions I made. Then, as I walked on, I realized I still did not hear footsteps. I wasn't walking on a concrete slab, but something better. I was walking through sprouts. Sprouts of trees. Sprouts of flowers. Sprouts of grass. All of the seeds I had planted were also experiencing the freedom to become what they were meant to be. What once had been only dirt and a concrete slab was now beauty; it was new life, and new beginnings...it was hope. This was my life; this was the beauty of the decisions I had made. This was my starting point. This was the day my life became my dream.

I saved some pieces of concrete. But I didn't save them because they were part of my story. They aren't. My story is created by the decisions I make. I did not pour the concrete. But I broke it! I saved a few concrete pieces because they remind me I can defeat anything. Their brokenness reminds others that they can win too. And, the concrete pieces remind me of the importance of seeds, of cheerleaders, of investors, and of belief.

Throughout this book, I want to share with you the three truths by which I now live. Each of them has amazing power. And each of them has massive importance.

ABUSE IS NOT MY STORY.
MY STORY IS CREATED BY THE DECISIONS I MAKE.
I DID NOT MAKE THE DECISION TO BE ABUSED.

Sometimes I will show you pieces of the broken concrete. But the concrete is not my story. I share broken pieces to encourage you that you are not alone. I share broken pieces to tell you that concrete breaks. You are not trapped. I share broken pieces so that you can touch them – so that you can feel them. So that you can see that the pieces don't have the power I once perceived they had. Maybe you still perceive the dirt is too full of decay. Maybe you believe the concrete will never break. I am here to remind you that it will break, and that you can shake off the dirt. And when light hits you – when you are drenched in it and when it takes over your soul – you will know that your story was worth fighting for. You are worth fighting for. So, let's fight.

Guided Journaling Activity:
Turn to pages 23–24 and Reflect on Concepts 1, 2 and 3

Chapter Two: Cracks

Abuse is not my story, but it was my experience. I can't remember how old I was when I was first abused, but I can concretely tell you that by the age of five I believed abuse defined me. The dirt and decay in my life eclipsed all other parts of my being. Abuse defined my behavior. Abuse defined my friendships – or, in my case, it defined my lack of friends. Abuse stunted my development. And, abuse snuck into my soul and set before me a belief that my life was not my own. In reality, I did not have a life. If a person's story is created by the choices they make, then my story did not exist. I was very obedient. I made zero choices; I obeyed out of fear. And, in the absence of having a story, I learned to believe that my experience was my story.

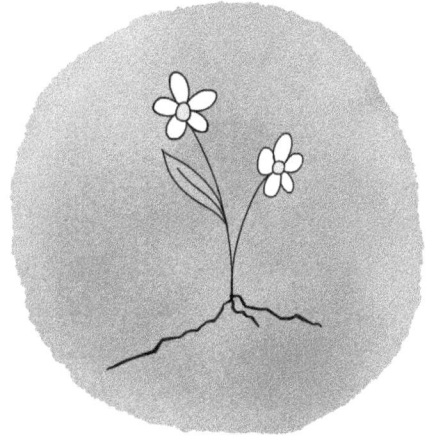

Living below the concrete defined me. I learned that I was separate. I learned that I was dirty. I learned that I was invisible. As my bones decayed in the dirt, I learned that one thing was consistent...pain.

In first grade all of my beliefs about myself were confirmed in one single instant. The day started much like any other. I went to school, hiding my pain, and wearing the smile I had been trained to wear. Things seemed normal – that is, until recess. At recess I somehow hit my private part on the playground equipment. In that instant, I knew my secret had been exposed. Blood escaped from inside of me. Despite all of my practice lying, I was not prepared to tell this story. So, I remained completely silent. I was sent home. There, instead of help, more concrete was poured. I became further separated from the life that I believed existed above the dirt. Isolation began to sink in. I tasted the dirt that had entered my soul. I realized that I would never be anything but dirt, and that one day I would decay, unnoticed.

This was only one of many experiences in my life. The reality of my experience is that it took me thirty-eight years to escape abuse. I had no reason to believe life would ever be any different.

If you have experienced abuse, there are some common characteristics connected to the dirt. One of them is that it may make you feel isolated. In fact, you may very well be isolated. You may even believe isolation is the only thing that keeps you alive. I am here to tell you that this belief is a lie. Abuse happens in the dirt. Abuse is often hidden from the public by a heavy concrete slab. In order to escape the dirt, you must begin to crack the concrete. The first crack is the scariest. It could be you didn't even intend for the crack to happen. That was my story.

By my 20's, decay had won. I had left college. The environment was more than I could handle. In the dorm, people joyfully reminisced about their childhood. Friendships formed. Relationships emerged. Dreams and future goals were frequent conversational topics. These things were not part of my dirt. Dirt was my life. The concrete slab between me and the things occurring in that dorm was thick. It was powerful. So, I buried myself further in the dirt.

My favorite isolation technique was studying. By the end of my first semester, my roommate needed out. My dirt was more than she could handle. I felt rejected. I grew further isolated. By the end of my second semester, I had confirmed in my mind that decay was permanent. I had been accepted into a sorority and had dropped out because I was different. I had entered into a relationship with a boy, but quit because I could not love. I had listened to stories of which I could not understand. So, I quit. I completely quit. I covered myself in dirt and invited decay to take over. And, it did. It took the form of an unexplainable illness. For days, I fainted each time I would force myself to walk more than a few steps. My arm shook – like a constant twitch. I had subconsciously assisted the decay by not eating most of my freshman year. Eventually, I was hospitalized for a few days, but the doctors found no cause for my symptoms. My body was shutting down, though. The decay was almost complete. The doctors recommended psychiatric help and evaluation. That never occurred. Instead I was moved into a new environment, and a new layer of concrete was poured to ensure that my decay would never be seen again.

That was not the first crack in my concrete, but it was the event that led to the creation of the crack. The crack occurred in a church. I entered covered in dirt, moments away from making the decision to let the dirt cover my mouth and nose to finalize my demise. For whatever reason, that day, I went to church. I sat on the back row because isolation from the experience is what my concrete slab demanded. But, that day, something unexpected happened. I cried. This was not normal. I was proud of the fact that I had not cried in years and years. Crying would have meant that I felt something. I felt nothing. But that day, I cried. My tears washed away a small amount of dirt; when that dirt moved, a small crack in the concrete formed. A cheerleader, who would later become an investor, noticed me below my concrete slab. My cheerleader let me know that life did exist above the concrete slab. The glimpse of life and the almost invisible ray of light gave me just enough hope to start creating my plan to escape. Would

it be possible that I could get out of the dirt? Could the death and decay that consumed me be reversed?

If you are living in the dirt today, below the concrete slab, I show you these pieces of my concrete for a reason. My concrete is broken, and I believe yours can break too. Abuse is not your story. Your story is created by the decisions you make. You did not make the decision to be abused.

In this chapter, I have presented to you three pieces of concrete. It is not until the third piece of my experience that a crack emerged. Healing is risky and sometimes it is hard to find cheerleaders. In my first two stories, a crack should have emerged. Someone should have cared enough to help me. But, they didn't. I don't know if they glimpsed at the dirt or if they just acknowledged that my life was dirty and walked away. But those days, they were not victories. They were defeats that further isolated me.

And this is where your fight begins. I know deep inside of you there is a belief that you can live out of the dirt. I mean really live; I mean experience the light. It could be that you were placed in the dirt as a child. Maybe today you are functioning but as you carry around your dirt – your concrete – you still know deep in your soul that you want to live.

Let's take the first step right now. You need a crack; you need a little dirt washed away so that someone will possibly see you. It is time to believe in yourself. You are worth it. Today, find someone with whom you can tell your experience. You don't have to feel the emotions of the experience. You might not be ready. But words are powerful. Saying the words breaks the silence. Saying the words could remove some of the isolation. Saying the words could move just enough dirt to destabilize the concrete slab. Could today be the day your first very small crack occurs?

If, like me, the first time your experience is revealed you do not receive help, remember this: Cheerleaders and investors are hard to find. But you are worth the effort to find them. They will challenge you, encourage you, and maybe help you believe that your life can begin. You, in turn, will inspire them. They will see in you what it really means to fight and their lives will be changed forever.

Telling your experience is not telling your story. Abuse is not your story. Your story is created by the decisions you make. You did not decide to be abused.

Making the choice to talk is your decision. Taking the first step to break the concrete is your decision. You are worth it.

Guided Journaling Activity:
Turn to page 25 and Reflect on Concepts 4 and 5

Milestone 1 Guided Journaling Activity
Hope Beyond Your Experience

Many victims of abuse struggle to find hope. Their experience of abuse is heavy and separates them from the life they long to have.

The first milestone centers around processing your experience and facing the pain that has held you captive.

Concept #1: Abuse is not my story

How has abuse shaped your life? Spend a few minutes journaling your thoughts.

_____

_____

_____

_____

_____

_____

_____

_____

_____

_____

_____

_____

_____

_____

_____

_____

Concept #2: My story is created by the decisions I make

Have you made a decision to pursue healing? Write out a commitment to break the power abuse has had in your life.

_____

_____

_____

_____

_____

_____

_____

_____

_____

Concept #3: I did not make the decision to be abused

Think about your abuser's actions, and journal your thoughts. As you do, remove any lies you have been told that the abuse was your fault or responsibility.

_____

_____

_____

_____

_____

_____

_____

_____

_____

Concept #4: No one helped me

Identify where have people failed to help you. How did the pain of that experience impact you? How have these feelings impacted your ability to heal?

_____

_____

_____

_____

_____

_____

_____

_____

_____

_____

Concept #5: Finding words to talk about my experience.

How would you describe your experience with abuse? Write it out as if you were talking to a trusted friend.

_____

_____

_____

_____

_____

_____

_____

_____

_____

_____

Milestone 2:

Partnerships on Your Healing Journey

Chapter Three: Cheerleaders

My cheerleaders have helped to change me. Their roles have varied greatly from cheerleaders who simply allowed me to experience life with them as a friend, to cheerleaders who cried with me and reminded me that the concrete would break. I have found that in my life the hardest part of having cheerleaders was actually just allowing them to be part of my life. Concrete has a unique ability to isolate, and dirt distorts your image of yourself. Fighting these obstacles while becoming vulnerable enough to have a cheerleader defies every lesson my concrete and dirt taught me. Yet, vulnerability is exactly where this conversation begins. Let me be clear, I am not telling you to tell every cheerleader about your experience. The vulnerability I am referring to could be as minor as making eye contact or maybe it is as major as listening to your cheerleader talk about their childhood while fighting a fear in your heart that they might ask about your childhood.

Let's establish a plan. First, I want to clearly define what I believe a cheerleader to be. Cheerleaders don't need to drop seeds into your dirt. It is possible that telling your experience to a cheerleader may be more than they can process. It is not that they don't care about you, but your experience may be too intense for them to internalize. Please understand... this is okay! Cheerleaders are not your counselor. They do not need to be your emotional sounding board. They are friends. They are people who can look at you and see the dirt that still surrounds you, yet their focus is on encouraging you that they care about you exactly as you are. They will and can be your friend exactly where you are in that moment. When you spend time with a cheerleader, you begin to see their definition of you is located in that moment, not in your past or your situation.

Having cheerleaders in my life has always been hard. Cheerleaders often saw a better version of me than I allowed myself to see. To be a friend to a cheerleader, I had to make a conscious decision to allow myself the ability to exist in that moment and enjoy the events that were occurring at that time. That is not how my dirt had taught me to function. My dirt gave me the ability to look around and see only one thing...more dirt.

My cheerleaders and I did "normal" things together. We went shopping, out to eat, swimming, and to church events. We experienced life, in that moment. As I began to allow myself to live in the moment with my cheerleader friends, hope began to emerge. My cheerleader could see a version of me that I wanted to exist. They saw an interactive, fun friend. My dirt still told me to be an isolated, unhappy person. Facing the challenge of two different views of myself was the greatest obstacle I faced in finding cheerleaders.

Finding cheerleaders can be difficult for other reasons also, though. My advice for looking for cheerleaders is three-fold. First, recognize that cheerleaders, like any other friend, can be seasonal. Your cheerleader does not have to make a commitment to be your friend until you die.

I found a lot of cheerleaders based on seasonal interest. It could be my cheerleader and I worked together for eight hours a day. I found some cheerleaders as I played recreational sports. Some went to my church. Others shared similar community interests. Start your search by evaluating your life. You won't find cheerleaders in isolation. Hopefully you do something outside of the home. Do you work? Do you play on a sports team? Do you attend church? Could you do some of these things? Start in one of the places mentioned. Begin small. A smile shared at work in the break room may be a great first step. One day that smile will evolve into a conversation, then a lunch invitation. Most of my cheerleaders do not know about the experiences I am writing about in this book. It could be that I intentionally never told them, or it could be that I was too scared to tell them. A few of my cheerleaders do know of my experience, but that is not the focus of our relationship. In either case, the cheerleader possibly saw some of my dirt, my concrete. It probably came out in awkward behavior I may or may not have even known I was showing. But the point is that my cheerleader accepted that awkward behavior and became my friend anyway. Their friendship with me existed in that moment, and not in the past.

One of the hardest things for me to accept was seasonality and depth. I had spent so much time below the concrete that I was starved for friendships. I fought an intense battle inside to connect and disconnect at the same time. My head told me no one would ever be my friend. I was dirty. I was different. But a small spark of friendship was enough to ignite in my soul a fire to want to consume and envelope anyone who might consider me worthy to be their friend. They liked me! They could cure my consuming isolation.

I needed to establish boundaries for myself. I hadn't had that much experience with friendship. So, I established these "rules" to help me:

1. My cheerleader and I will be the ones to decide if we should become friends. I will contribute equally to the development of becoming a friend but if the friendship does not develop, I will not internalize it as a loss. If I contributed equally, then the fact that it did not fully develop was just the reality of that encounter.

2. Different cheerleaders will have different depths. One cheerleader may simply be fun to have lunch with periodically. Another may be my movie buddy. And another may become a constant buddy I talk to almost daily. I don't need all of my cheerleaders to play the same role. But, all of my cheerleaders will break my isolation.

3. Cheerleaders may leave. This boundary was difficult for me to accept. Seasons change; this is the reality of life. My work buddy may be gone when I leave for a different company. My workout friend may decide she likes to swim instead of lift weights. Lots of friendships end. When they do, I must focus on being grateful for their existence. I must recognize that the friendship helped me grow. And, I must let go. I can contribute

my part to developing the friendship in a different setting, but if it doesn't remain, I must be grateful that it once existed.

The second piece of information I had to remember about my cheerleaders is that my cheerleaders are human, too. My cheerleader will make mistakes. My cheerleader will possibly hurt my feelings. My cheerleader may even intentionally hurt my feelings.

The humanity of cheerleaders causes me to once again face a vulnerability that is completely unnatural for me. As I lived in the dirt, under the concrete, I listened to life above me. I heard footsteps of anger, busyness, and joy. Yet, the concrete blocked my view of what that actually looked like. Because of my inability to actually view life, I wrongly believed that the life above me was perfect. It isn't. As cracks began to emerge and I began to interact with cheerleaders, I realized that their lives had complexities too. A cheerleader may have at one time (or many) been hurt. A cheerleader may have experienced things that formed their belief system. That belief system might be different from mine, or it may be very similar. The point is: My cheerleader is human. My cheerleader is not perfect. I do not need to place them upon a pedestal as something I want to become. Instead, I need to extend to them the same grace that they have extended to me. I need to live with them in the moment. I need to recognize that they may also wear some dirt. I need to realize that each cheerleader is unique and different and that his or her individual traits are a treasure.

One of my cheerleaders has been on a journey with me as I discovered and accepted that she too was human. We met at church. I entered into the Sunday school room only after having had a full panic attack. Small groups and personal connections were very uncomfortable for me at the time. She saw me and motioned that I could sit by her. Within minutes, the beliefs of my dirt had taken over. I did not belong amongst this group. I began to cry and left the room to collect myself. When I returned, she acknowledged me as a person, not my dirt. She simply asked me if I wanted to sit with her in church. Immediately she was placed on a pedestal of perfection in my mind. Over time she became one of my closest friends.

We learned to live life in the moment, enjoying daily activities. My trust in her was high. Much later, we faced a topic we intensely disagreed about. I firmly believed I was right, and she firmly believed I was wrong. During the encounter, she hurt my feelings deeply. She unintentionally attacked my identity and made me feel unimportant because our value systems were different. This was one day where our friendship demanded that I realize that cheerleaders are human. I still loved her, and she was still my cheerleader/friend. It would have been unfair for me to expect her not to be human and have a human response to a topic we intensely disagreed about. In the end, she apologized... but before her apology, I had already forgiven her and had begun to move forward in my mind.

Allowing your cheerleaders to be human is very hard. I had already lived in the dirt. I had no interest in becoming vulnerable enough for someone to ever hurt me again. I felt protection in isolation. Allowing a cheerleader to become my friend would break the isolation, but I feared I might get hurt again.

Survivor, the vulnerability I am talking about is healthy. Cheerleaders will help you learn to live in the moment, not in your past. This trait is critical to your ability to live life when your concrete breaks. It will be hard. You will be scared. You are worth it. Your life is created by the decisions you make. You must decide that vulnerability is worth the risk. Your cheerleader did not make the decision to abuse you. You have to treat them based on the decisions they make, and release them from being responsible for the consequences of the decisions another person made.

Finally, the third thing you should remember is that your cheerleader is an individual. You need to be you, not them. You and your cheerleader are not a "we."

I hope that your life is filled with lots of cheerleaders. I hope that some of those cheerleader relationships are deep, daily friendships. But, Survivor, do not ask your cheerleader to fill the void that exists in your life. Do not look to your cheerleader to complete you. It is likely that a part of your heart is still searching. You could be searching for a "mom" who will love the little girl you once were, or for significance to remind you that your abuser's harsh words were wrong. Maybe you are searching for love that you believe will complete you. These are wounds. They were established in the dirt.

The problem is this: No human – not even a cheerleader – can heal these wounds. Frequently survivors find themselves in unhealthy relationships because they are looking to another human to heal the wound.

I believe there are two things that fill my wounds. First and foremost, I believe that only the One who created my heart can heal it: Jesus Christ. Jesus understands wounds. He stands victorious with two gaping holes in His hands. I believe that only in Him will your heart ever heal. Second, I believe your heart can experience temporary joy as both you and your cheerleaders live in the present and embrace acceptance, love and confidence. The things that you have searched for are found as you interact, as you love, and as you belong. Your experiences will temporarily relieve the pain of your wounds. You will feel better, but remember that these feelings and fun experiences will not fully heal your wounds. That role is reserved for Christ. Do not ask your cheerleader to "fix" your heart.

Cheerleaders are valuable. They are treasures. You are a treasure to them also. Being vulnerable enough to find cheerleaders will be your first challenge. So let's start the process now.

Take a piece of paper and write categories in which you function. For example, a few categories for me are Mom, believer, employee, boss, and Sunday school teacher. Next, below each category write down everyone you interact with. These people do not need to be your friends. Third, write down how you interact with that person today. It could be not at all. For example, there are people who work in my building whom I don't even say "hi" to.

Next, set goals. Decide on a few people that you will develop this week. It could be that your first step is just to make eye contact or say "hi" to someone in your work break room. But decide what progress you will make this week and hold yourself accountable to it. Next week set a different goal. Continue until you have developed a cheerleading team.

Let me take one step back. It is possible that you may need to practice this week's assignment. If so, here is an assignment that my counselor gave me to help me prepare for the above assignment. Begin by realizing you might not even be looking beyond yourself.

At the time I was given this assignment, I did not really even acknowledge people existed. I was completely isolated in my own world. My assignment was to go to the grocery store and look ten people in the eyes and say hello. It was terrifying. By dragging my dirt and concrete around with me, I had believed people lived in the same world as me yet I had no interaction with them. So, my first assignment was to move into the moment long enough to say "hi" and make eye contact. It is okay if this is your first step.

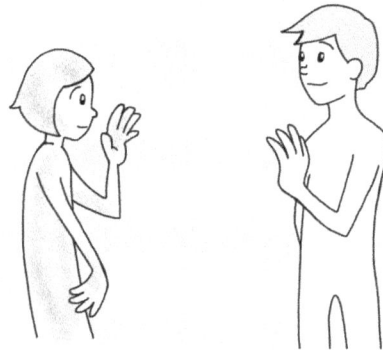

Survivor, don't forget to celebrate. It is a big deal to look a potential cheerleader in their eyes. Having lunch with a new friend may feel enormous. Whatever your step, you are making progress, and you are worth it.

Guided Journaling Activity:
Turn to pages 57-58 and Reflect on Concepts 1, 2 and 3

Chapter Four: In the Moment

In the last chapter, I connected cheerleaders and living in the moment. For many survivors the concept of living in the moment is distant, unrealistic, or even unknown. The moment may have even been a scary place in your past. You may have learned to psychologically leave the moment to control pain, to minimize experiences, or simply to imagine a place of peace.

Let's start by defining what it means to live in the moment. Living in the moment means that physically, emotionally, intellectually, and spiritually you are experiencing the stimuli that exist in the place in which you are located. It requires that you slow down; it requires that you allow your senses to digest the occurrence. It requires trust and safety. You must be willing to be present, and to trust yourself and those with you. You must be safe enough to "feel" your surroundings.

Today's culture is not good at living in the moment. Survivors struggle even more than most to find the moment. Many survivors carry around their concrete and view only dirt. These obstacles prevent them from seeing the moments that are occurring around them. For some survivors it is such a struggle that psychologists have labeled it Post Traumatic Stress Disorder or PTSD.

But, Survivor, I have fought the journey. I have broken my concrete. I can experience life, today, in the moment. You can too. It will take guts and lots of practice, but it is worth it. You are worth it.

Before we focus on how to live in the moment, let's talk about why it matters. Do you remember the feeling of living under the concrete? Are you living there now? Do you remember listening to footsteps above the concrete? Can you still hear them? Let me ask you a question: What happens when the concrete is gone? How will you live above the dirt? The skill of living in the moment is a skill that must be learned. It will likely be uncomfortable and even frightening. But this skill is mandatory. When your concrete is gone, you don't want to fall back into covering yourself in dirt because it is the only place where you are comfortable. Learning to live in the moment occurs one small step at a time. This skill, however, is imperative for you to master in order to embrace the freedom that is your future.

After a couple of years of counseling, it occurred to me that I had no understanding of what my counselor was talking about when she asked me how it felt when I did something (insert any number of life experiences here). Experiencing each "moment" in my life was unknown territory for me. Functioning inside of a task made sense. Checking things off my checklist made sense, but digesting and internalizing things was not a skill I possessed.

As we evaluated my starting point, I realized that I had ignored most of my senses. Not only was I not living in the moment but I also had actively blocked the experience of the moment from my mental processing. Together with my counselor we created a plan – some details of which I will challenge you to experience.

Initially I needed to focus on reminding my undeveloped senses that they had a job. I practiced listening deeply by utilizing earth noises like crashing waves. I needed to train myself to remember that noise occurred around me, and I had the ability to listen to it and not just block it. When I felt safe, I took my resurrected listening skills to real life experiences. I went outside and heard birds chirping. I actively listened as leaves rustled.

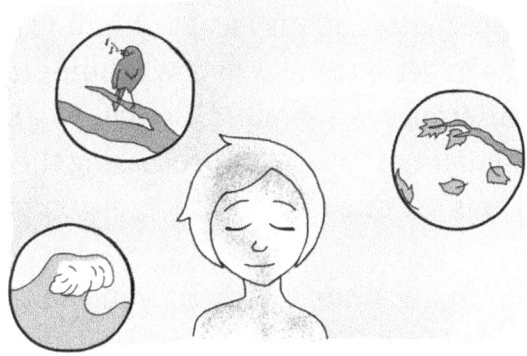

This sounds easy, right? NO! Listening doesn't always involve peaceful noises of nature. I remember going to see a doctor around the time I was learning this concept. In the waiting room, I heard the news blaring on the TV, two sets of people carrying on different conversations, someone on the phone, and the receptionist rustling papers. There was way too much noise for me to process. In the past, I would have heard none of it and just focused on being inside of myself. But that day I heard every noise. I couldn't process it out. By the time the doctor came, I was shaking and trying hard not to cry. He asked me what was wrong, and I told him. After the visit, he called my counselor very concerned about my behavior.

Acclimation to living in the moment may be difficult but it is worth it. I continued my journey with touch, smell, sight, and taste. I experienced one of my biggest victories while driving to work one day. I wasn't intentionally trying to be present in the moment, because I was driving. But, both sides of the road were lined with beautiful trees. The sun was beaming through the trees producing magnificent light rays. As I drove I became overwhelmed with the beauty of the scenery. I had driven the road for years but had never noticed what surrounded me. All of my senses tuned in and I was able to be fully present in that moment, enjoying the radiant scene.

Being present in the moment is closely connected to intentionally experiencing the moment. My children and I just finished a summer full of experiences at our local swimming pool. There were times when the joy of the experience was overwhelming, and there were times I just swam. The difference was simple. Sometimes I made the decision to be present and sometimes I was still processing the events of my work day. In both cases, I was the one making the decision to experience the moment, or not.

From these stories I hope you can see that living in the moment is simply choosing to live – to be. For me, this choice occurs intentionally. If I don't remind myself to live, I will just function. Many of my survivor friends have shared a similar need to operate intentionally. I believe this need may be present for all people regardless of life experiences.

Why should you live in the moment? This answer is really simple. You fought (or are fighting) hard to be able to live above the concrete. Let's live! Let's not only shake off the dirt and break the concrete to be able to function. Let's be intentional. Let's experience life. Let's feel sun hitting our faces, and laugh with our children until our belly hurts. Let's run through the rain.

Getting started is simple. I recommend seeking out a quiet place, so you are not overwhelmed with unnecessary stimulus or distractions.

Once there, take some time to listen. Right now I hear the refrigerator humming, the air conditioner clicking on, and electricity – or something I can't quite identify – making a white noise. Once you've spent some time actively listening, transition to touch. Where are you sitting? How does it feel? How does each of your body parts feel against the surface? Spend some time internalizing the different textures, and digest what you touch. When you are ready transition to each of your other senses. Stop and sit in each of them. Can you hear something new? Do you smell something good...or bad? Can you see something differently than before?

I recommend that you do this exercise many times, in many different quiet places. When you are ready, try it (or portions of it) in a more demanding environment. Eventually challenge yourself to experience everything you can around you for five minutes. As you become more comfortable, increase your time.

There are many additional ways to experience the moment. Some people love visualization. Others illustrate their experiences through artwork. Some write, and some record songs. Once you have learned the basics, try different things! Mostly, live.

Guided Journaling Activity:
Turn to pages 59–60 and Reflect on Concepts 4, 5, and 6

Chapter Five: Investors

Many of the people whom I love the most in this world found me while I was buried below the concrete, in the dirt. They made a choice to acknowledge me – concrete, dirt and all. They knew they were taking a risk that my dirt might get on them, but they made this choice because they cared about me. They intentionally handed me seeds through the concrete. They watched to see if I would plant those seeds, and they reminded me that there was hope. The seeds would grow.

My first counselor introduced one of my early investors to me. She made the choice to invest in me. She probably did not understand the depth of the choice she was making, but she desired to watch me experience freedom in whatever time frame God had for me.

I honestly don't remember the early days. At that time, the act of telling about my experience was stressful and brought up trauma I really wasn't emotionally ready to process. But I am confident that somewhere along the way I must have told her about my abuse experience.

In the early days, her investment in me was largely one of love and belief. At that time she loved me and believed in me more than I believed in myself. She encouraged me to see myself as someone who was worth love and possessed value.

Although I don't remember our early communication about my experience, I do remember the day I showed her a very large piece of concrete. As we talked, a crack emerged, and it felt horrible. I felt exposed, and the fact that I had talked produced a vulnerability that I detested. I remember her coming to my work and hugging me while reminding me that it would be okay. I told her that it absolutely would not. I had been crying for two days, and I would never be able to stop.

Twenty years later, I can tell you that I actually did quit crying. Showing my investor pieces of my concrete eventually became less painful. I learned that she could be trusted and that she would accept me for whom I was, despite my past experiences.

Showing my investor pieces of my concrete was not the only interaction that occurred in our relationship. My investor and I engaged in fun activities. We watched my children and her grandchildren play together, as her husband played guitar in another room while we talked. We prayed. I shared my dreams with her. She showed me stability. She stood beside me in hard times and did not judge me for my lengthy healing process.

Not all investors are long term like the one I referenced in the above example. Like cheerleaders, investors have seasonality. I am eternally grateful that I was given a long-term investor, but I am also grateful for those who have been in my life for shorter seasons and purposes.

Let's take a moment to define what an investor is and is not. An investor is a mentor – a deep friend. Investors possess the internal ability to accept themselves but also share a part of themselves with you. Your dirt does not define them, and they are comfortable with the fact that you have dirt. They are able to reach deep within you and challenge you to see and believe things about yourself that you may have forgotten or never believed.

Investors, by definition, will go deeper with you than your cheerleaders will. But, please remember that your investor is not your counselor. They will support you, listen to you and love you. But you will still need a counselor to help you dissect the experiences you have had, create a healing plan, and renew your mind with positive thought patterns. Yet, I also want to be true to my own experience by adding that a good counselor may also be an investor.

Sometimes investors have no knowledge of your abuse experience. A large, seasonal investor in my life was also one of my bosses. He really defined intelligence. He was Harvard educated, yet had a trusting and gentle approach to business. He believed his employees could be successful and was willing to invest extra time in our development. He taught me to believe in myself, and my ability to run a business. He challenged me to grow and never settle for anything less than my full potential. The lessons he taught me could be applied to every part of my life and extended far beyond the business world.

Investors, like cheerleaders, are gifts. Investors, like cheerleaders, are hard to find. Investors, like cheerleaders, will change your life. And, you will impact theirs, too.

Building a relationship with an investor is similar to building a relationship with a cheerleader. We must be grateful for the time investors are in our lives. We must realize some relationships will develop and some will not. We must accept that boundaries in the relationship will help keep both of us healthy. But there is one thing I am passionate about that must intentionally and specifically be done with an investor: We must acknowledge their role in our lives and take the investment they are making seriously.

Your investor has likely taken a very thoughtful approach to how they have invested in you. Their advice, their observations, and their love should be something you consider. I am not telling you to always take their advice or agree with their observations. I am telling you to consider them. Your investor loves you; they are intentionally spending time with you. Consider what they are saying and determine how you will respond.

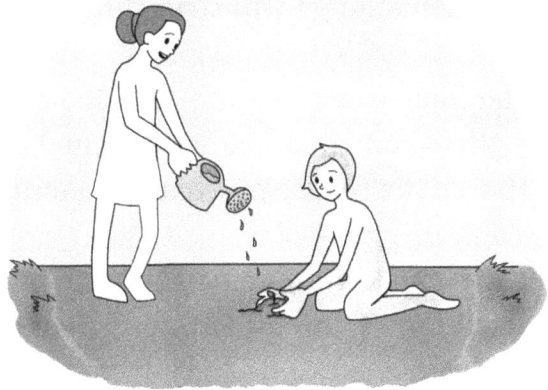

I know this may sound basic, but I wonder if it really is. You see, you may be (and likely are) coming into your investor relationship wounded. You want to be relieved of the pain you are experiencing. You feel and experience the depth of caring your investor is offering. The emotion is important, but it is only part of the experience. The other part is the life-changing seeds. Little nuggets of wisdom for you to plant, to nurture, and to watch grow in your life.

Finding an investor can be difficult. You should not expose your experience to everyone that you meet. Sometimes the investor will see you, and despite your concrete they will choose to look at you. Other times we have to tell the investor we need them.

I have a friend in my life that is very capable of being an investor or a cheerleader. Depending on the situation, she will rotate between the two roles. Our relationship began because I told her I desperately needed her. At the onset of the relationship, I really was just looking for a conversation, a moment of hope. She blessed me with so much more.

I watched my investor for many months. She faithfully served in the nursery of our church. Her smile and positive attitude was contagious. I was going through a particularly hard situation in my life. I was not handling it well. I needed someone to talk to. So, I took a huge risk. During church I wrote a note and I asked her if she would be willing to have lunch with me and talk about something I was struggling with in life. She agreed.

Later that week, we ate cold food. It had once been hot food, but the length of conversation had resulted in what was now cold food. I cried as I shared the reality of what was going on in my life.

At the end of the conversation, she graciously looked at me and said something to the effect of, "I hear so much hope in your story. Your dependence on God is inspiring." WHAT! Did she hear the same story I was telling? Hope? Dependence? I questioned her. What had she heard that I did not hear myself say? The answer was that she heard my heart.

She did not focus on my words or my despair, but she looked at the love and dependence that underlined my story. She heard my heart.

This was one example where I had to apply my rule about acknowledging my investor's insight into my life. As I allowed myself to begin to see in me what she saw in my heart, hope emerged and healing began.

Sometimes insightful attempts to find investors work. Be careful that you do not miss the word insightful. In the last story I had watched my investor for an extended period of time. I did not know that she would become my investor, but I did have a belief that she was a genuine person who could be trusted. I was correct.

Other times investors will find you. I recently had a friend at work tell me that she thought I should meet a friend of hers. This friend had once been my friend's investor and still served in that capacity from time to time. Initially, I did not want to meet her friend, but I am beginning to learn to trust myself enough to take a few risks. I decided that this was a risk I would take.

The friend of a friend connection led me into the path of a great investor who had faced many of the same challenges I have faced in life. Had I not been willing to be vulnerable to a stranger, I would have missed out on a huge blessing in my life.

Finally, investors might be found in systems, such as mentoring programs and developmental groups. Even an event might be what introduces you to investors.

I met one of my investors at a healing event. She and I both attended as participants. Almost instantly, I knew that my attendance at the event was not a coincidence. I believed that meeting this investor was the reason I had attended the event. Over the next few years, our friendship continued to grow as we both learned how to heal, and were intentional about sharing what we had learned with one another. We made intentional choices to remain positive and to allow the other person to benefit from what we were learning.

Survivor, as you begin (or continue your effort) to find investors, be wise. Think about the type of person you will allow to invest into your life. Be intentional about finding people who have the same belief system or worldview that you have. Recognize that relationship development will occur sometimes, but other times it will not. And if you have investors currently, be grateful. Tell them that their presence in your life is a blessing and that you do not take what they do for granted.

Finally, if you absolutely cannot find an investor, invest in yourself. Make a confidence journal. Write in it the things you see in yourself. Read books. Discover your passions. Journal about your experiences.

I want to be clear: All of the above recommendations are good, but people are important. Invest in yourself, but do not quit looking for investors. You will find a people investor if you continue to look.

Guided Journaling Activity:
Turn to pages 60-61 and Reflect on Concepts 7 and 8

Chapter Six: Counselors

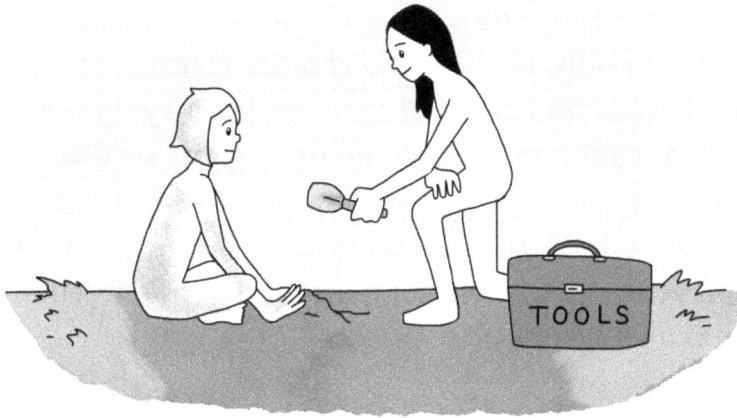

Initially, when I began writing, I imagined discussing the importance of counselors in the investor section of the book. However, as I wrote, I realized that the importance of a counselor necessitated its own chapter.

Let me start with a very adamant belief that all survivors need a good counselor or counseling team. I am aware that this statement may be hard to execute. Finding the right counselor for you may be a difficult task. I hope that this chapter will enable you with some tools to evaluate what a good counseling fit might look like. Additionally, I believe survivors must understand their responsibility in maintaining the counseling relationship, as well as counseling boundaries that are established to support a healthy relationship.

So, why do we need counselors? Because concrete is difficult to break, and dirt and decay can hurt; a counselor can be a consistent cheerleader and investor, and we need to learn to live when concrete is broken – mostly because we are worth it. Counseling, for me, is one of the ways I constantly prioritize myself. Yes, it can be expensive. Yes, it does take time. And yes, it requires a long-term focus on growth.

If you have experienced significant abuse, counseling is not a short-term commitment. A good counselor will not promise that you will feel better quickly. My counselor actually challenged me at the beginning of my journey. After many visits on an unrelated topic, I decided to share with her the details of my experience. I noticed her facial expressions changing as I talked. I ask her why. She said that healing is sometimes painful, and she wondered if I really wanted to begin the process. She respected me enough to be honest and truthful that the journey would not be easy, but she was also willing to support me through it. Survivor, I encourage you with the same knowledge. You deserve to heal. I encourage you to be brave enough to heal. Healing is not easy, but it is always important. Living beyond your experience is important. Finding freedom to become uniquely you is a journey worth pursuing.

Second, the act of starting a counseling journey is an action step, which communicates to yourself that you believe in your worth. So, how do you get started? I encourage you to consider the following:

1. Where have I seen success? My current counselor had counseled one of my employees before she became my counselor. This employee shared openly about the progress she was making in her life. Before meeting my counselor, I had the beginnings of confidence that she could probably help me also.

2. Recognize that good counselors may require you to wait. When I first called my counselor, she was not accepting new patients. I shared with her my referral's name and asked if I could be placed on a waiting list. In my mind, I had decided that I would wait up to six months. (There is no magic in this number; it is simply what I decided I was willing to do). My wait ended up being significantly shorter than six months. To this day, I am pleased that I was patient to secure the right fit for my counseling needs.

3. Remember, you are never trapped. Sometimes you believe you have found the right counselor, but as your visits progress, you realize the situation is not a match. Just be honest. Your counselor is trying to

support you. They have likely dealt with this before and could possibly even give you a recommendation of someone who might be a great fit. I went to a counselor one time many years ago. She was intelligent and quickly identified my need for safety. Her approach was aggressive, and her desire was to help. I, however, was extremely insecure and needed someone to win my trust slowly. Neither of us was wrong; we were just incorrectly matched.

4. Recognize that there are many counseling approaches. I did not understand this at all when I began counseling. Do some research and so that you understand how your counselor was trained. You need to be comfortable with the approach they will take with their counseling. Also, realize that in addition to the many different styles of traditional office-based counseling, there are many alternative types of counseling. I have a friend who has focused her journey on art, body, equestrian, and somatic counseling. I have really enjoyed hearing about her journey and watching her apply her natural creativity to the healing process.

These thoughts, along with basic filters, will help you find the right starting point for your search. Don't forget the basic filters that technology has simplified for us. Check reviews of a potential counselor online. And don't forget to review coverage that your insurance may provide.

Finally, I want to pause here and recognize that urgent needs require urgent help. If you are severely depressed, suicidal or unsafe, please seek immediate help. Your situation does not allow you the time for a thorough selection process. You may even find that an inpatient facility or emergency room may be required to ensure your protection. If you are in this situation, prioritize the immediate care that you need. If, when you are stabilized, you believe a change is needed to optimize your growth, discuss this with your counselor and allow them to help you identify next steps.

After selecting a counselor, your journey begins. The most important thing I can tell you about your counseling journey is this: it is a shared journey. You and your counselor are on it together. Your counselor is not leading and you are a hurt survivor doing as you are told. NO. You will be mutually contributing throughout the healing journey. Please note that I did not say you were equally contributing. There will be times one person contributes more than the other. This is true of all relationships. However, when you evaluate the journey as a whole, you will see that there have been mutual contributions that have allowed you to achieve the milestones you have reached.

I recommend that you begin your counseling journey by sharing about yourself, and seeking to understand your counselor. What does your counselor enjoy most about their job? Why did they decide to become a counselor? Have they worked with other clients who have backgrounds similar to yours? As you share about yourself, think about how you would like to approach your journey. Do you have specific goals you would like to achieve? Are there things about your experience that you believe it would help your counselor to know before you begin? Why did you decide to pursue healing?

Your first few sessions are about trust. You must understand one another. Your counselor may establish some boundaries; you may have some to discuss also. Be open to wherever the conversation leads; you are learning to work together.

As your counseling journey progresses, it will be important that you understand your responsibility to your counseling success. Counseling is not a one-session-per-week commitment. You may actually only have one office session with your counselor per week, but that session has follow-up responsibility. At a very minimum, your responsibility is to process what occurred during your session. Again, you and your counselor are on a shared journey. You do not have to blindly accept what she may have said during a session. What did you learn about yourself as you heard yourself discuss the topic of the session? Are there negative beliefs that you still struggle with that may no longer be true? If your counselor made comments, do you agree with them? Are there things that you can learn from his or her statements? These questions, and many more, are examples of minimum processing you should do after leaving a session. You have to let counseling challenge you. You have to be willing to reflect and grow.

Many other activities can be done outside of counseling to enable the maximum benefit from the relationship. Ask your counselor their recommendation on "homework assignments." Early in my counseling journey, I journaled frequently. I was very uncomfortable with my whole experience. Writing became a personal way for me to acknowledge the experience in a very safe setting. I had complete control over what topics I wrote about and could express my vulnerability through writing, as I felt appropriate. My counselor also asked me to work through reading workbooks. The books that we used had short chapters and workbook-style questions. The power of this exercise was in taking the extra step of personal reflection. These exercises also allowed me to mentally prepare for whatever emotional vulnerability might be required as I processed the content during our session.

I give you the above examples as early counseling assignments. But I want to note that your counseling assignments will reflect your counseling stage. After my concrete had broken, my assignments changed. Some of my assignments centered on "feeling" the world – and allowing myself to exist in it. For example, touching leaves may seem small; but, for me, being in the moment, feeling the leaves' veins, and embracing how the leaf felt on my skin – these behaviors required significant vulnerability. Looking strangers in the eye and saying "hello" developed confidence that I was missing. Responding to peoples' small talk required me to acknowledge that my words might matter, even to a stranger. My point is that your assignment matches your place in your journey.

Work with your counselor to establish your assignments. This is a joint journey where you are mutually contributing. Your counselor is equipped to help you set proper assignments; how intentional you are with these assignments will determine the impact they will have.

Finally, I want to add that it is very important to work with your counselor to create healing goals or visions. But, I encourage you that it is important to respect their position as an expert. They have led others down the journey that you are on. You have the benefit of what they have learned on other peoples' journeys.

There are two areas where I have seen many people struggle to respect a counselor's position as an expert. First, survivors may feel the need to diagnose themselves. Second, they may pursue understanding and reading about this diagnosis at inappropriate times. Survivor, you began this journey to heal, not label. There is no label that will change your current situation. Your experience is individual. If you read about ten different people with the same diagnosis you have, they likely will have had ten different experiences. You may have had similar behaviors, but you are not putting a Band-Aid on your behaviors. You are healing from an experience you have had.

My counselor set two boundaries with me in the early days of counseling. I respect these boundaries and encourage you to strongly consider them. The first one was: no research. I did use the Internet to conduct research. I did not read books, unless my counselor had recommended them. I did not research. I lived my life. We were meeting to discuss my experience. The details of my experience are personal. I did not want to take the risk of mixing up details of my experience with details of something I had read.

I am so grateful for this boundary. One of my core beliefs is about the importance of truth. I am so grateful that this boundary allowed me to heal from my experience, and prevent questions, unnecessary processing and stress from an experience that was not my own.

The second boundary my counselor recommended early in my journey was to focus on milestones and progress, not on the diagnosis. This was an intentional boundary to allow me the freedom to define for myself who I am and not allow a label to define me. I am good at making hard choices. I am determined to heal. I am a very good mom...and many more things! But, I am not a label. As you reach milestones and experience heart changes, you will begin to understand yourself. You will begin to find pride in what you are becoming. You are more than a behavior or a label. Survivor let me be clear; it is likely you will have some diagnosis. I do. But diagnoses only define behavior. Of course you have some different behaviors. Your experience forces you to live below concrete, in dirt. My encouragement in this boundary is let your journey be about healing. Your behavior will change as you wash off dirt. You will begin to see a beautiful person. And, if there is a behavior that does not change, you can address it further in the journey when your counselor believes it is appropriate.

Your counselor will have other boundaries. Take time to understand why the boundary exists, not just what it is. You may also set your own boundaries. If you do, explain to your counselor why the boundary matters to you. Finally, realize that boundaries at one stage of your healing journey may not be necessary at another stage of your journey. Today I can hear about other people's experiences. Today I can read about my own diagnosis. I can do both of these things without letting them define me, causing me to question myself, or potentially internalizing data that is not mine. I will be clear, however, that I don't do either of these actions very often. I don't need to. I fully understand my experience and my diagnosis. Nothing I read will change who I am, so reading without a purpose becomes wasted time. Abuse is not my story. My story is created by the decisions I make. I did not make the decision to be abused. I did make the decision to heal. I did make the decision to understand myself.

I hope that the few pieces of information I have placed in this chapter will help you evaluate your healing journey and your healing partner – your counselor. As I shared in both the cheerleader and investor chapters, please remember that your counselor is also human. They will guide you with your best interest in mind. They will never intentionally hurt you. But, they are human. If something does not feel right, talk to them about it. Sometimes communication resolves issues and clarifies next steps.

Throughout this chapter, I have given you many questions to ask yourself. Take time to evaluate the questions that fit your stage of the journey. If questions do not exist for wherever you are on the journey, establish your own. Pursue homework. Counseling is a commitment. Growth is a lifelong way to invest in your life. Periodically remind yourself that your journey is about intentionality. Are mutual investments occurring on your journey? Are you maximizing learning and growth opportunities along the journey?

Guided Journaling Activity:
Turn to pages 61-62 and Reflect on Concepts 9, 10 and 11

Milestone 2 Guided Journaling Activity
Partnerships on Your Healing Journey

All survivors can benefit from a team of supporters – cheerleaders, investors, and counselors. This milestone evaluates how to grow these relationships, and yourself, along the healing journey.

Your second journaling milestone will challenge you to maximize the relationships that exist in your life.

Concept #1: Cheerleader relationships require trust. . . in myself and in my cheerleader

How would taking the risk of finding or growing cheerleader friendships help you in your healing journey?

_____

_____

_____

_____

_____

_____

_____

_____

_____

_____

_____

_____

_____

Concept #2: Vulnerability may be uncomfortable for me

Do cheerleaders or other people in your life see a better version of you than you see of yourself? What prevents you from having more cheerleader relationships?

_____

_____

_____

_____

_____

_____

_____

_____

Concept #3: I will establish a starting point

Identify three ways you can grow specific cheerleader friendships. How will you make sure your expectations of these relationships align with the boundaries in this chapter?

_____

_____

_____

_____

_____

_____

_____

_____

Concept #4: Living in the moment requires trust and safety

Do you feel specific emotions that make living in the moment difficult?

_____

_____

_____

_____

_____

_____

_____

_____

_____

_____

Concept #5: Living in the moment will prepare me to embrace the freedom that is my future

What opportunities do you believe you will miss if you do not learn to live in the moment?

_____

_____

_____

_____

_____

_____

_____

_____

_____

_____

Concept #6: I can intentionally choose to live in the moment

Recall your last experience living in the moment. What was it, and why was it impactful for you?

_____

_____

_____

_____

_____

_____

_____

_____

_____

Concept #7: I am considering my investor's input in my life

Who is investing in your life? Are you embracing the opportunities they offer, or are you so inwardly focused you are missing opportunities to grow and heal?

_____

_____

_____

_____

_____

_____

_____

_____

Concept #8: I am investing in my healing

Some activities in life generate hope and promote healing. Ideas mentioned in the chapter include: spending time with investors, considering their advice, making a confidence journal, reading, and discovering your passions. How are you planning investments into your healing? Is there an opportunity for you to be more intentional in this area?

_____

_____

_____

_____

_____

_____

Concept #9: All survivors need a good counselor

Trust is important in counseling relationships. If you have a counselor, evaluate your trust in that person. If you are searching for a counselor, what steps will you take to build trust into the relationship early?

_____

_____

_____

_____

_____

_____

_____

_____

Concept #10: Counseling is a shared journey

How are you and your counselor mutually contributing into your healing journey? What steps could you take to more intentionally embrace your counseling experience?

_____

_____

_____

_____

_____

_____

_____

Concept #11: Prevent distractions

Your healing journey is a path to gain freedom from your experience with abuse. This journey is about your heart, not your behaviors. Are you engaging in activities that may be distracting you from healing? Are you focused on fixing behaviors or healing your heart?

_____

_____

_____

_____

_____

_____

_____

_____

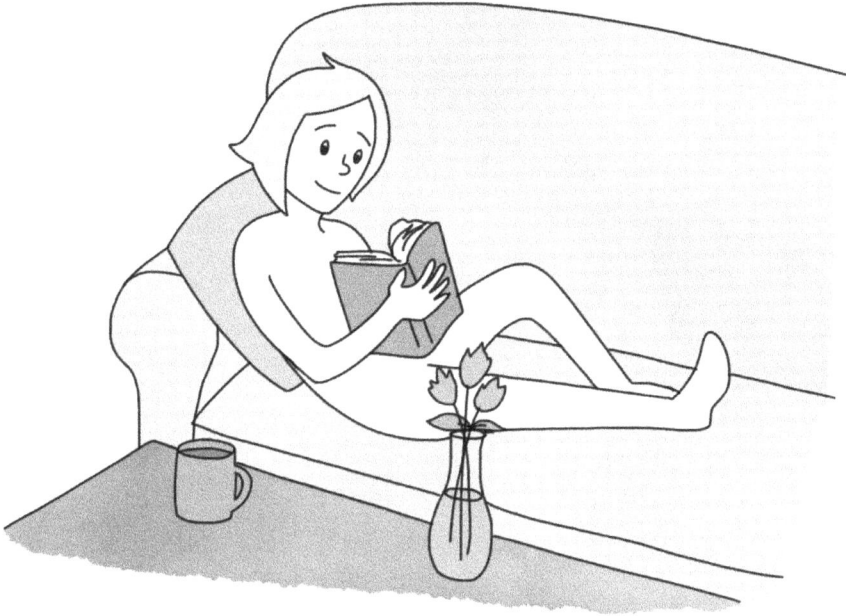

Milestone 3:

Creating an Atmosphere to Grow

Chapter Seven: Small Cracks

A few times in my career, I have had the opportunity to take underperforming organizations and help them heal and produce again. I believe the transformation I watched in those businesses had many traits similar to my personal healing process. Intentionally oversimplifying the process, three things must occur. First, the organization needs to acknowledge that healing would benefit them. Second, the leader must acknowledge and celebrate small steps – these are directional and give hope to the organization that it will achieve its goals. Third, the organization must persevere. It must allow many small changes to produce a large, impactful movement toward health.

I guess I feel like those three intentionally oversimplified steps illustrate a survivor's journey toward healing. The survivor must first decide that they want to heal, and that healing is important. They must become vulnerable enough to acknowledge their brokenness. As they begin the process of healing they must be intentional about celebrating victories. Healing does not occur overnight. Without milestones and times of celebration, the journey may seem too long. The endpoint may be fuzzy and the vision that creates hope may be weak. We must recognize progress and success occurring in the moment, and not focus exclusively on the end. And, finally, we must realize that in the end, the sum of many small victories will be what creates lasting, monumental change.

I would like to share with you a few pieces of my concrete. These pieces, however, reflect cracks and seeds. These pieces reflect some of the power that caused the concrete to break.

Let's start with acknowledgement. It was intensely hard for me to decide to acknowledge my brokenness. I wanted to believe I was okay. I wanted to believe that I could make my pain go away by simply working hard at "being normal."

I started counseling in my 20s. I was blessed with a counselor who genuinely loved me and wanted me to experience life abundantly. Over time, we made progress. We faced a few really hard issues, but I did not yet have the inner strength to expose all of the dirt and decay in my soul. When things grew really hard, I ran.

My experience with this counselor was not lost. My time with her was a treasure. I experienced the early stages of seeing my brokenness and allowing someone to love me despite my dirt. At that time, the biggest problem was that I did not love myself, or have enough confidence in myself, to face the healing process.

Acknowledging that you are broken takes guts. It feels like once you expose your brokenness and need for help that you might fall apart and never be able to be okay again. Acknowledgement somehow requires a shred of belief that concrete can and will break.

By my 30s, I had ridden the roller coaster of life. There was a lot of good, some bad, and a nagging knowledge in my being that I still carried concrete and dirt everywhere I went. I actively tried to convince myself that I could be okay without acknowledging the dirt and decay.

But I guess life has a way of reminding a person when they are wrong. By my mid-30s I had entered counseling again. During this round, my intention was to deal with an issue completely unrelated to my experience with abuse. Today my counselor lovingly recalls her early experiences with me. I had a very limited capacity to engage with her. My answers were almost robotic and my mannerisms made it clear that we would go no deeper than the exact issue for which I had sought counseling. That was really my approach to life. Don't interact – just function, and function well so that no one sees your dirt.

The problem was that there was a lot of dirt. The dirt pressed into me. I did not have space for the new dirt this life situation had brought. And, when the new dirt combined with the existing dirt, I could no longer breathe. I told my new counselor that there were some things about me I wanted to share.

Acknowledging my brokenness was painful. Trusting someone with the knowledge of my experience was unnatural. Yet, that vulnerability is one of the milestones of my healing journey. I wasn't really acknowledging my brokenness to my counselor. I was acknowledging it to myself. It wasn't my counselor I was trusting with the details of my experience – it was myself. I needed to look at and acknowledge those details. And, somewhere deep inside this acknowledgement came an attached feeling of hope. I had to now embrace the hope that existed inside of me, and believe it could actually be for me.

Stage two of my journey has a multitude of milestones. Concrete breaks; lots of cracks in the concrete help.

Some early changes I noticed in myself were not associated with meeting a goal; they were found in willingness. I was willing to be vulnerable in counseling. It was hard. I was willing to journal and write feelings I had previously ignored completely. I was willing to allow myself periods of brokenness. I sat in my pain – but now, for the purpose of ending it. And, I was even willing to ask for help. I shared very small pieces of my dirt with my investors. I allowed them to see the real me and choose to love me no matter who I was.

If you are starting your healing journey, the willingness I am talking about is significant. It is a heart change. It is almost a belief system change. It is moving from the belief system that you have the power to cure yourself, to the belief that help and healing may require more than just your determination to be okay.

Early milestones aren't all pointed at an action-based, goal-specific experience. Start instead by celebrating your heart. By celebrating that in your heart, you know there is hope, willingness, brokenness, and belief.

Finally, don't get too anxious for the end result. I don't know when healing ends. I honestly am not sure that it will ever be complete until we reach heaven. But, I am confident of this. Lots of small victories equal enormous, mind-blowing explosions in your concrete. My concrete is broken; I have washed my dirt off. Hundreds, maybe thousands, of cracks and milestones felt the eruption when my soul finally yelled a victory scream as my concrete was blown up.

Today my healing process is focused on living above the dirt. I am experiencing the flowers, the grass, the trees, and the beauty that surrounds me. But I haven't finished. My healing simply has a different venue. I still celebrate small milestones. I can look back and see all of the small changes that have created the healthy, productive environment I live in today. I know my future is bright. I know that challenges I face today will be milestones I remember in the future.

Survivor, I encourage you to begin, to celebrate, and to grow! I don't know what place you find yourself in today, but I do know that if you don't intentionally exist you might become discouraged. You could even abandon your journey.

Evaluate yourself briefly by asking the following questions:

- Do I believe that it is important that I heal? Or am I still focusing on merely surviving?
- Have I given myself the freedom to celebrate what I feel my heart becoming? Or am I focused on curing troubled actions?
- Can I allow others to celebrate with me?
- Even if I do not know my end destination, can I celebrate that many milestones have significantly changed me?
- Could I allow myself to be patient along the journey of healing?

I encourage you to journal about the questions above. It is not self-motivation. Write your honest answers, even if they are ugly. Write what your heart believes. A milestone in your life might simply be to do the same journaling exercise again in three months. You may find your heart is opening up. Maybe you celebrate your willingness, your commitment, your determination, or your desire. There is something about you that is absolutely beautiful. Today, I celebrate that! Today I celebrate that you are committed enough to read. Today I celebrate that you are strong enough to journal.

Guided Journaling Activity:
Turn to pages 81-82 and Reflect on Concepts 1, 2, and 3

Chapter Eight: Living Below the Concrete

In this chapter, I want to break from the concrete analogy. But, don't worry. The break will be momentary, because there is so much more to tell about the dirt, the concrete, and the ability to break it and be drenched in light. But, for a moment, I want to challenge survivors to evaluate their dreams and look at their lives.

Thus far, I have referred to concrete and dirt from an emotional perspective. As a survivor, you have likely at some point in your life felt the emotions of the dirt: decay, invisibility, dirtiness, impending death, isolation, and many more. You have probably struggled to breath below the weight of concrete, an experience that separated you from what you believed life could be – the inability to ever break through despite your sincere efforts, the belief that the weight would actually crush you.

Survivors need to be taught healing techniques. This book isn't really focused on coping techniques. But, I can tell you they are intensely important. Coping techniques can help you stabilize when the concrete and dirt are more than you can handle. For this reason, and many more, I recommend that all survivors enter counseling. If you cannot afford counseling, there are many great books that can help you learn to cope.

But, let's talk about today. Maybe you have taken a huge step toward creating a crack in your concrete. Maybe you have told your experience for the first time, the fifth time, or the fifteenth time. Now it is time to look inward. Behind every crack is a dream, a belief that life can be different; it is the smallest feeling that maybe what I am saying is right – maybe you are worth it.

There isn't really a secret place below a concrete slab that survivors live. But the emotions of the dirt and concrete are something survivors live every day. My life has always looked great to an outsider. I learned early on that a huge smile would alleviate any suspicion that life might not be what the smile said. I learned that silence and obedience would keep adults from getting to know me. As I grew older, I refined my techniques. Really hard work, good grades, and a confident smile would help me to be labeled a "good kid." And, being a good kid kept me safe. It didn't matter that I was really dirty and worthless. As an adult, I learned to apply my techniques to succeed in business. My whole life, I functioned. As long as my concrete wall could keep me separate, as long as there were no questions, as long as I had no real personal interaction, I would be okay. I never had to feel anything; I just had to function.

The survivor life for me was isolation. My isolation technique was invisibility. I didn't have a heart technique. I just learned not to let it feel. I didn't have a friendship technique; I just kept everyone at a distance. And I definitely did not have a purpose technique because I felt I had none. What I did have was a small hope somewhere deep inside me that I was wrong – a hope that maybe all of those things could be for me.

My pain medication was being "good" – at least good enough to function. Some survivors choose a different path. Some survivors seek unhealthy, potentially abusive relationships because they believe this will help them feel like they belong somewhere. Surely someone cares about them. Surely someone can break them out of the isolation of the concrete and dirt. If you are a survivor who has chosen belonging techniques like your drug buddies, your newest partner, your gang friends, or whatever, I invite you right now, in this exact moment, to realize that this is your medication of choice to cure isolation. But this is not your problem. Your isolation, your pain, your feelings of worthlessness, your secrets – these are your problems. You will never find what you are looking for in "medications." They just cover up the problem. My success "medication" left me feeling just as empty as your "medication" leaves you.

What can fill you up? What can crack your concrete? What can begin your healing is resolve and dreams. I believe we were all created in the image of Christ. And, in Him there is completeness, acceptance, and power. So, if we are created in His image, how do the dirt and the concrete exist? I plan to share with you pieces of my concrete that answer this question for me. But, for now, let's not focus on "why." Instead, let's focus on "what." What is it in your heart that you still believe? What is it in your heart that you still hope for? What could your life look like if you finally found out who you were?

The first time I took out my journal and attempted to answer these questions, I sat hopeless. I knew deep inside me that I hoped to one day live, but that hope seemed so unrealistic that I couldn't even convince my brain to imagine a future. This was another time I wanted to bury myself in dirt and encourage decay to occur as quickly as possible. But, I am stubborn, thankfully, so I kept asking and asking myself the same questions. I remember standing in my house, touching a pole that separated my living and dining rooms and walking in a circle, holding the pole, chanting, "I am a robot. I wake up. I go to work. I come home. I work more. I go to bed. I do it over and over. I am a robot." The idea that I would dream was just stupid. People like me didn't have purpose. People like me just exist until eventually we die.

My brain must have finally grown tired of me wasting time on the same questions, because eventually, a dream emerged. My dream was that I would help others live a better life than I had lived. I did not believe that there was hope for me to live that better life, but I believed it was possible for others. And, just maybe, I could help them find life. Today, I get it. That was a pathetic dream. I still didn't believe one thing for my life. But it was an amazing starting point. I had something to focus my life into. I lived in that very small dream for a long time. I learned to dream on behalf of other people. It gave me something to live for.

You have to have a starting point. You need to dream. Maybe you already dream, but your dream is too small. Maybe you only can dream for other people. I don't know where you are at, but I know you have purpose.

You don't have to exist only below your concrete. It is time to open your brain to the concept that there might be more. You might have a really cool purpose. You might change the world. You might be someone else's cheerleader or investor. How will you know until you take the risk to dream? I believe in goals. I believe hope can be found in purpose. I believe your dreams and your purpose are connected.

It is time to take out a notebook and ask yourself three questions: (1) What do I want? (2) Why do I matter? (3) What is my dream, and how can I take a step right now toward that dream becoming reality?

You did not choose to be abused. You don't have to let your abuse experience isolate and define you. Your story is created by the choices you make. You get to choose to dream. You get to choose to live. You get to choose to watch your dream break your concrete. You did not choose to be abused, but you do get to choose to live.

Guided Journaling Activity:
Turn to pages 83–84 and Reflect on Concepts 4, 5, and 6

Chapter Nine: Boundaries

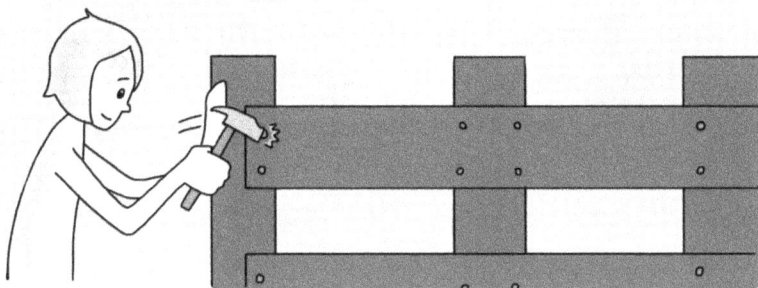

Growing up in unsafe atmospheres presented me with the option to internalize two extreme boundaries: no boundaries and rigid boundaries. If I learned from my abuser's behavior, I learned that no boundaries existed. Hurting, invading, experiencing at another's expense, and experience itself trumped all. However, if I learned from my abuser's words, boundaries were extreme, rigid. I was to be separate. No one was to know about me. Closeness was dangerous. Growing up in unsafe atmospheres prevented me from learning that boundaries differ from relationship to relationship and from time to time.

Moving into my adult life, these extremes translated into very black and white thinking. I know some survivors embrace no boundaries in hopes of experiencing acceptance, even if only for a moment. I went to the other extreme. Concrete separateness, in my mind, had translated into security. Yes, I was stuck in dirt – I was decomposing – but blocking everyone from my experience had to be safer than being hurt again, right? Yes, I was lonely. Yes, I was still dying. But I wasn't hurting...right?

Wrong. I mastered the act. I had a perfect smile that would convince anyone I was happy. But I was dying. I was looking for safety. My extreme behavior of pushing everyone away was also pushing away my ability to experience life. I could not break my concrete because I needed it to shield me. I needed it to keep me separate.

Survivor, I don't know how you have processed boundaries in your life. I do know that you were taught unhealthy ones. The act of abuse is an unhealthy boundary. Boundaries are about respect: respect for others, respect for yourself, and respect for the world. People who abuse dismiss respect and adopt a mentality they are the only ones that matter – only their emotions and desires are important. This mentality is unacceptable.

I don't know if learning about boundaries as an adult is a different experience than learning about boundaries as a child. I do know I needed lots of guidance. I do know that I am still learning. And I do want to share with you a few core concepts from what I have learned.

Boundaries are found in compassion, in self-respect, in a desire to promote health and safety, and in a desire to bring clarity. None of these concepts can be fully developed in dirt; so, if you are still on your healing journey, realize that you are also still on a journey of growing and becoming better at making good boundary decisions. This healing journey is a lifelong process.

There are a couple of tools that I have used to create my boundaries and evaluate other people's boundaries. The first one is "the pause." Can I discipline myself to pause long enough to view the boundary through the lenses of compassion? Can I take time to relate and view the boundary through their eyes? What about self-respect, will this boundary cause me to feel negatively or positively about myself? Does it align with my value system? Is it good for me? Finally, is the value promoting health and safety? Is it a wise decision? What does the boundary tell me about the relationship I am in?

These questions take time. It takes time to realize the importance of asking them, and it takes time to become skilled at the second tool, which is communication. Communication and boundaries are closely connected. I have seen communication play a critical role in all of my relationships. I want to tell you about two.

I have a friend who struggles with communication. She is a very black-and-white thinker, and often statements she makes can feel judgmental. She also struggles to see the world through other's eyes because her value system tells her it is black or white. She is also a great friend. She listens well. She genuinely cares, and she believes the best in me. Her friendship is important to me. So, I had to learn to pause, to process what she was really trying to say instead of just what the words were, and to communicate. Her black-and-white thinking often came with boundaries attached. I learned to restate what I thought she was saying the boundary was and open communication as to why it mattered and if I agreed. I also learned that sometimes communication revealed that what had been said was not a boundary at all, but a miscommunication. Finally, I learned to set a boundary and verbalize when I was uncomfortable and needed a conversation to end. In this example, I think those boundaries and the communication about them have strengthened our friendship.

Sometimes, however, boundaries are non-negotiable. This was the case with some very important people in my life. The basis of trust requires boundaries. In this case, the people I am referencing did not have good boundaries. Unfortunately, this led to people getting hurt, including myself. I worked with these people for an extended period of time to create and communicate acceptable boundaries. When hurt entered the relationship, my boundary had to become rigid and unmovable to protect my family. I put the boundary into writing and explained the steps that would be necessary to change the boundary. One step was that the people had to acknowledge and admit the pain their actions had caused. In this case, not only did that not occur but also the lack of boundaries and the inflicted hurt became more dangerous for my family. I created another boundary, and put it in writing, to prevent further damage from occurring. At this time, many years later, we still do not have a relationship with these people.

I want to pause here to bring out a very important concept. Sometimes boundaries are painful but they never harm. Here is the difference. In my last example, termination of the relationship was painful, emotionally. I mourned loss. I mourned the loss of the dream of what the relationship could have been. I mourned the investments I had placed into the relationship. I even mourned the hurt in the relationship and the fact that I had not been able to resolve it. I assume that the people on the other side of the relationship also mourned. I know they wanted things to be different, but the relationship was unsafe. This is where the difference between pain and harm becomes important. The pain I am referencing is compassionate, hopeful, emotional pain. It is the pain of an unrealized or un-experienced dream. Harm, on the other hand, is a negative physical or abusively emotional experience, which comes from a lack of boundaries. Survivor, allowing yourself to be consistently or periodically harmed is a choice. You must make the choice to end it. Create a boundary that acknowledges that your health and safety is more important than a negative relationship. The act of abuse is an unhealthy boundary. You deserve more respect than that.

Let's pause for one more moment. Children in abusive experiences do not have the tools to release themselves of a situation. Their abusers do not respect their needs for boundaries. Many organizations have been formed to protect children and others who need it. I pause here to remind you, Survivor, not to hold yourself responsible for abuse that occurred in your childhood. You did not have the tools to protect yourself, and the abuse was not your choice.

The final tool I wanted to mention here is that boundaries are hard and may require lots of sacrifice. In the second example I shared with you, I lost more than just a relationship. Our family had to move; we had to change cars, jobs, and phone numbers. For a time, we had to become aware of our surroundings and be watchful that our new situation was safe. There are a lot of emotions that go into such a dramatic change. Candidly, for a time, I felt no peace or freedom in our new life. I felt trapped by having to be watchful. Today, I can tell you that the sacrifice of a very hard time period was worth it. My family is safe. I am able to relax and focus on being a good mom. Peace will follow sacrifice.

If your boundary is of an extreme nature, know that organizations exist to help you stay safe. Do not stay in a harmful relationship because you believe you have no options. You do. Your life may be disrupted for a time, but eventually you will regain stability.

In less extreme situations, boundaries still may require sacrifice. You may find that there are events in which you cannot participate. Friendships may fade away, or communication may feel uncomfortable. But realize these sacrifices, too, will stabilize in time. The boundary will become something that brings pride because you respected yourself and your situation enough to do the right thing.

Survivor, I conclude with a reminder that boundaries take time to learn. Boundaries are different in every relationship. Boundaries also change over time. But, good boundaries open the door for vulnerability...healthy vulnerability. Good boundaries provide you with the opportunity to challenge yourself, the opportunity to learn about yourself and others, and the opportunity to experience safety and compassion in life. Boundaries also allow you to learn vulnerability in communication. They allow you the opportunity to verbalize something and learn that it can be respected or challenged in a way that still respects you as a person. Finally, boundaries can give you the freedom to protect yourself and embrace the value of self-worth.

I encourage you to begin with two key relationships. Evaluate each relationship from your perspective and from theirs. Identify boundaries that exist, and be willing to challenge the relationship in areas where you can grow.

If you are still at a point in your healing journey where you have not allowed yourself to experience significant relationships, you can do this exercise with work relationships, neighborhood relationships, or simply your relationship with yourself. Maybe you can identify areas in your relationship with yourself that are preventing you from growing new friendships.

Boundary work is hard. Be patient with yourself. Your boundaries will become more defined as you experience the world and gain a confidence to function inside of it.

Guided Journaling Activity:
Turn to pages 84–85 and Reflect on Concepts 7, 8, and 9

Milestone 3 Guided Journaling Activity
Creating an Atmosphere to Grow

The optimal environment for growth enables survivors to celebrate and dream in a safe and secure environment.

Your third journaling milestone will help you evaluate how to best optimize your growth environment.

Concept #1: Acknowledging brokenness takes guts

What made you decide the pursuit of healing was worth the pain of facing your brokenness?

_____

_____

_____

_____

_____

_____

_____

_____

_____

_____

_____

_____

_____

_____

_____

_____

Concept #2: Celebrate small steps

What heart changes have you experienced on your healing journey? How can you intentionally celebrate those victories?

_____

_____

_____

_____

_____

_____

_____

Concept #3: Persevere, and never give up!

How has the sum of many small victories created monumental change in your life? If you haven't experienced monumental change yet, journal about your dreams of what that day will feel like.

_____

_____

_____

_____

_____

_____

_____

_____

_____

_____

Concept #4: The ability to dream is powerful

How has your experience with abuse suppressed dreams you hold? Can you declare today that your abuse experience will lose and you will dream again?

_____

_____

_____

_____

_____

_____

_____

_____

_____

Concept #5: I have a purpose

What do you want in life? Why does your life matter?

_____

_____

_____

_____

_____

_____

_____

_____

_____

_____

_____

Concept #6: My dreams and my purpose are connected

What is your dream for your life? How can you take a step today toward your dream?

_____

_____

_____

_____

_____

_____

_____

_____

Concept #7: The act of abuse is an unhealthy boundary

How has your experience with abuse challenged your ability to feel safe? How has it challenged your ability to feel respected?

_____

_____

_____

_____

_____

_____

_____

_____

Concept #8: Characteristics of healthy boundaries

The book states that healthy boundaries are found in compassion, in self-respect, in a desire to promote health and safety, and in a desire to bring clarity. What challenges do you face in establishing healthy boundaries in your relationships?

_____

_____

_____

_____

_____

_____

_____

Concept #9: Boundaries may be painful, but they never harm

Are there harmful relationships in your life that are preventing you from growing in your healing journey? How can boundaries protect you in this situation? If you are not in any harmful relationships, what relationships in your life could benefit from better boundaries?

_____

_____

_____

_____

_____

_____

_____

Milestone 4:

Understanding Your Purpose

Chapter Ten: A Moment of Pause

Survivor, I want to pause and share with you details of the experiences you will read about in the next three chapters. For some of you, these chapters will be the hardest chapters in this book. Please read them anyway. You see, complete healing can only be found in Christ. Yet, as a survivor, that statement was unimaginably hard to feel. God wanted things, like trust, that I did not know how to give. And, I was mad at Him. After all, He controls the world. Why didn't he help me?

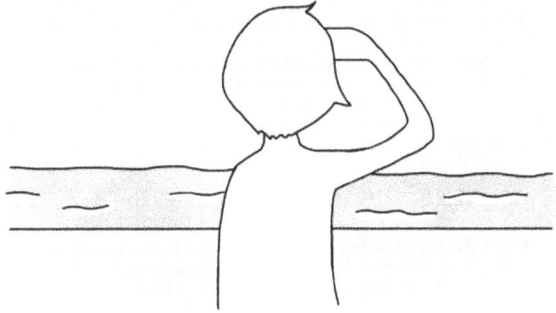

The next three chapters were written during very different phases of my life and my desire to know God. The thought patterns I had during these chapters will show you transitions that occurred in my willingness to know God. I considered editing these chapters to share the story the way I would write it today, but in the end I decided that it was more important for you to feel the stages that I experienced on the journey.

The chapter, "Where was God" was written in a season of belief without experience. I genuinely believed the words of the Bible. My belief was so strong I was even angry with God at times. I would tell Him things like, "I read in the Bible that a lady touched Jesus' garment and was healed. I believe this happened and that you can do it. So, why won't you? Why can't I instantly be healed?" I used many different Scriptures to point out to God that He had the power to do things but that He just wouldn't. I didn't feel like God cared enough to do it for me. Reading this chapter will feel academic. My experience with God at that time was just that – academic. I believed but not was experiencing, understanding, or living in relationship with God.

As you transition to "The Love of the Father," you will feel the Lord saturating me with the love He has for me. You will see me beginning to understand that the connection between His love and my life was His son, Jesus. It wasn't just Jesus' death, but it was Jesus' life that changed me. While writing this chapter, I still did not understand or fully connect but I was feeling and beginning to see love. It was after I wrote this chapter that I surrendered my life and embraced Christ's love.

The final chapter in the group, "Attachments," was written during a time of spiritual healing. The love of Christ was real, and I was positively overwhelmed by His presence. I did not know how wonderful the journey of knowing Him would be, but I did know I was choosing to experience it every single day.

Abuse, overly strict rules, and my own interpretation of life led me to believe God to be powerful, but distant and uncaring. I believed Jesus to be mad at me because I was bad. I carried these beliefs for many years. It wasn't that I didn't want the love of Jesus, because I did. I wanted it desperately – but it seemed like it just wasn't for me. I wasn't acceptable.

All of those beliefs came from the dirt. They weighed me down like tons of heavy concrete. All of my beliefs were false. Today I live fulfilled. No matter how hard this topic is, it is the most important.

Guided Journaling Activity:
Turn to pages 109–110 and Reflect on Concepts 1, 2, and 3

Chapter Eleven: Where Was God?

The question "Where was God?" is almost a default question that I expect people to ask as they process the detail of my experience. How could a loving God allow me to be hurt so badly? Why didn't He stop the situation? Where was He?

I guess I wonder if all of these questions don't reflect more about me, more about my flawed belief system, and more about my pain than the story of God. Let me try to explain.

We were born into a broken, sinful world. In the book of Genesis, God tells Adam and Eve that their sin will separate them from the deep, vulnerable relationship with Him that they had experienced in the garden of Eden. He tells them that life will be hard. Abuse is unfair. But, I don't think that God ever promised us a broken world would be fair. I do think that in my brokenness my need for a Savior is excessively evident. I do think that the unfairness I have experienced will be shockingly contrasted when I arrive at a perfect heaven. I won't tell you that I wasn't broken by evil people, and in ways that are impossible to understand. I won't tell you that what happened to me was okay. But I will tell you that the desperate cry of my broken life is exactly the need that drove me to a point of surrendering to my Savior.

God gave us a free will, a choice. He desires for us to be like Him, in His image. Yet, beginning in the garden, He allowed us the freedom to make that choice. In the garden there were many good gifts – many trees provided blessings. There was also a tree to be avoided – a tree we were asked not to touch. Somehow, even before the trees were created, God knew. He knew He would give us a choice. He knew we wouldn't always make good choices. He knew that our bad choices would separate us from Him. He knew the only way to resolve this disconnect would be through His Son's death, the payment of His life for our choices. And, He still gave us a choice. We have the choice to choose good or evil. We have the choice to be separate from God or to actively live in a relationship with Him. We have the choice to accept the reconciliation Jesus' death offers.

Our abusers were given these same choices. Our lives are created by the decisions we make. We did not make the decision to be abused. Our abusers did make the decision to abuse us. That is their story, their choice. A loving God, who gives us the ability to choose to accept Him or reject Him, also extends this choice to our abusers. There isn't a magic line where it is okay for us to make certain choices and not make other choices just because that choice is too bad.

Noah lived in a time of corruption but Noah chose, however, to follow God. God used him to tell people that judgment was coming, that a flood would destroy the world. God even had Noah create an enormous boat that visually represented the people's ability to choose life or death. Everyone who did not climb on board the boat chose death. They made a choice. God didn't wake up one day in a fit of anger and destroy the world with no warning. Instead, He lovingly waited as a boat was built, a message was delivered, and choices were presented. There were no power drills. There was no machine to speed up production. People watched as a boat was assembled board by board. Those who did not enter the boat made a choice.

So did your abuser. No one has to be an abuser. They make a choice, a choice to hurt someone. They may have even made that choice multiple times. Let's remember that we need to place the responsibility of choice on the person who made the choice.

However, God is always present. It is really hard for me to imagine God or Jesus being present when I was abused. It seems easier to think that somehow He was absent – that somehow He lacked control in a chaotic situation. But God's Word clearly states that He has loved us with an everlasting love and that He is drawing us with His lovingkindness (Jer. 31:3, NIV). The Bible says that He stands at the door and knocks, and that He seeks for us to allow Him in. These verses, and so many more, reference a God who wants to be part of our life, every minute, every day. He isn't so shocked by bad choices, by evil, and by abuse that He has to be absent. But He is willing to be in the middle – the core – of our broken existence on this earth. He is willing to let His everlasting love consume us. He is willing to abide in our hearts. He is willing to bring us stability today. He is willing to bring us hope. And, He is willing to offer us an eternal home that will have no sin, but instead completeness, and where we will celebrate Him for eternity.

There are a number of ways I believe that I see evidence of Christ's presence in my abuse experience. First, my ability to survive points me directly to the one who placed that ability inside of me. When a person is experiencing trauma, their brain, their behavior, and their whole being adapts. An example of this adaptation for me included memory suppression. I simply can't remember large portions of my experience. It would have been too much for me to process if I had to live daily with the reality of my situation. So, I forgot. In my case I even established rituals that I used to help me forget. I believe that this was a blessing. Another adaptation technique I used was submission. As a child, I needed to be obedient to remain safe. My obedience was extreme, unhealthy. The people I obeyed were evil and wrong. But in my experience, fighting would have produced more traumas. A third adaptation technique I used was belief. In the darkest hours of my life, I possessed an unexplainable hope. I believed that my world would change. I interacted with the world through a lens of optimism. Deep in my soul, I knew that my life was worth more than what I was experiencing.

I want to be clear. First, these were not all of my adaptation techniques. Second, these techniques were not all healthy. Techniques that allowed me to survive trauma had to be evaluated again as I began to break my concrete. When a small level of safety had been achieved, I had to learn again how to function in a world that was not characterized by trauma.

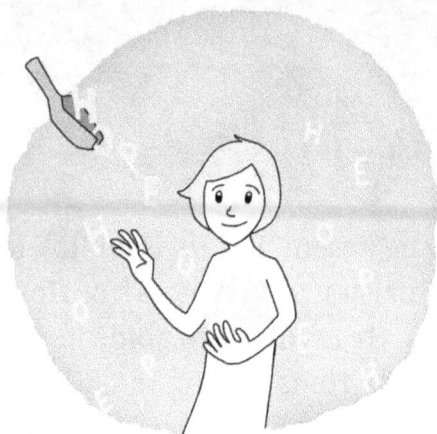

My survival shows that the power of God is greater than the power of evil. My ability to adapt and minimize pain was a creative gift given by God to allow me to recognize brokenness and recognize evil, to feel its impact but not become permanently disabled by the evil itself. This hope that has no human explanation was a gift from God Himself. I wasn't yet ready to accept His eternal gift, but He pursued me. He loved me with an everlasting love. He reminded me that I was made in His image. He waited until I was ready to embrace His love and let Him transform my heart into His home. And, finally, my healing reflects His completeness. There is only one way in which I can be complete. God created me to commune with Him. The connection and fellowship He established with the creation of Adam and Eve began with His breath literally being breathed into our existence. Without acknowledging His existence, without experiencing a small glimpse of who He is, I would never experience love. Love and unconditional acceptance brings completeness and healing.

Maybe you have rejected God. Maybe you blame Him for actions performed by your abuser. Maybe you are in so much pain you just can't imagine anyone wanting to love you. Maybe, just maybe, everything you have believed about Jesus is wrong.

He made the choice to create you. He desires to interact and fellowship with you. He knew you before you were created in your mother's womb. Your days were not a secret from Him. He will sit with you in pain; He did.

Jesus felt the pain of your experience when He was separated from God on the cross. Jesus felt the pain of your experience when He paid for the cost of your abusers' sin.

I know He desires to be a part of your life. You have lived without the completeness Christ brings for long enough. The only love that is complete and unconditional is found in Him.

The Bible says, "If you declare with your mouth, 'Jesus is Lord,' and believe in your heart that God raised Him from the dead, you will be saved" (Romans 10:9, NIV). You can begin to fellowship with the One who completes you.

Abuse isolated you. You felt alone. You believed you were alone in the dirt. The reality is you were never alone. Jesus has been waiting, loving, and longing to embrace you and love you in a way only a perfect God can do.

Guided Journaling Activity:
Turn to pages 111-113 and Reflect on Concepts 4-9

Chapter Twelve: The Love of a Father

I love my children. I believe they are the biggest blessings of my life. My children return this love to me. They love me, and they trust me to take care of them.

One of the things that is important in our home is bedtime and the bedtime routine. I believe that sleep is important for my children's physical, emotional, and spiritual development. Our bedtime routine consists of several tasks – like brushing teeth – and quality time – like reading. The kids sleep in their own beds.

My daughter loves her mommy. She can never get enough hugs, being held, and interactive time. After she started school a new pattern emerged. Each night she would wake up, sneak to her mom's room around 2:00 am, and go back to sleep. When I woke up three hours later, I would find a little munchkin asleep on her side of the bed, happy. I didn't stop her 2:00 am trips. I was curious to see if they would continue.

The next phase of her 2:00 am trips emerged in a prayer. She said, "Dear God, please make sure I wake up in time to go to mommy's bed." This prayer continued for a couple of years, but after a couple of months, I could hold my curiosity no longer. I said, "Lizzy, how do you feel when you come to mommy's bed?" Her smile almost exploded. She said, "So excited!" Remember, I am asleep. She does not wake me up. The first time I know she is there is the next morning when I wake up. When I see her, my first action is usually to give her a hug while she sleeps. I have to admit; I feel a little of that "so excited" emotion myself. I like the fact that the first thing I see in the morning is one of my favorite people in the world.

As this little "sneaking" routine continued, I decided to find out why it was occurring. I knew it wouldn't last forever because as she grew older, I was aware the pattern would change. But, I was still curious why in her mind she wanted to wake herself up in the middle of the night and come to my room. Throughout several conversations I learned that it began with nightmares. She believed she would be safer with me. As I taught her to pray for peace over her sleep, the nightmares left but the behavior continued. She later told me that she just loved to be with her mom and going to my room was one of the best things in her life.

My love for my children pours out of every part of my heart. I believe that I love them with all of the capacity I have to love. Yet, I am also aware that I am a human who lives in a broken world. Even while pouring out all of the love that I have to offer, my love for my children doesn't even compare to the love a perfect, complete Father has to offer you.

Lizzy loves to be with me, even when I am asleep. Lizzy believes she feels safety, just because I am near. God's love is so much more than I could ever offer Lizzy. God desires to be with us all of the time. He knows how to be with us at work. He protects us and sits with us as we drive. He wants to be part of your life everywhere, every day.

I love the verses that say that God has loved us with an everlasting love, and He has drawn us with His lovingkindness (Jer. 31:3, NIV). Because of Jesus' death, the only thing that can separate us from the love of God is rejecting Jesus. He is aware we make mistakes. He is aware we might even do bad things on purpose from time to time. But once we have confessed that Jesus is Lord and believed on Him in our hearts, God no longer sees our mistakes. Instead, He sees them covered by the blood Jesus shed on the cross.

If you have not confessed Jesus as Lord, I want to point out the phrase He "has drawn" us with His lovingkindness. I love the fact that the word drawn is in past tense. God has drawn me to Him throughout my entire existence. During my abuse, He was drawing me. During my healing, He has drawn me. There is never a point in which He has not drawn me to Himself. Like Lizzy, the God of the heavens and the earth wants to spend time with me. He wants to be near me. He likes it when I feel secure because He is close.

A lot of things cause us not to feel this drawing of the Lord's love. Noise, busyness, pressures and more consume our lives in ways that we don't hear God. If you aren't sensing the love of God, slow down. Go to a quiet place. Talk to Him. Read about Him. There have been times I have even yelled at Him. He already knew how my heart felt, so we talked about it.

When you feel God's love, there are really two responses. First, if you have never felt His love, your first response needs to be to...respond. Remember, God gave us choices. We have to choose Him. He stands at the door of our heart and knocks, but we have to choose to invite Him into our lives. The second response is to want more. Allowing God to love me has been really hard. I mentioned in the last chapter that, for me, the creative ability to adapt and survive is evidence of God's protection of me. I also cited that all of my adaptation techniques were not necessarily healthy once I was safe. I am very good at feeling nothing. I am very good at trusting no one. I am very good at pushing away anyone who wants to love me. I believed that all of those traits protected me. The problem was that I did all of the above to God. When I finally believed that Jesus was Lord and I confessed Him with my mouth, I experienced an overwhelming love I had never experienced before. I wanted to feel that emotion – that connection to love – every day. But, I didn't know how. And soon, I pushed the love of God away. To be clear, God never stopped loving me. I still was a Christian. He still was the King of my heart. But I had to learn, and am still learning, to let Him love me, to live in His everlasting love. I had to learn to acknowledge it when I saw it in my life. I had to learn to trust it when I needed to feel it in my pain.

God's love is and will always be part of your life. Some of you will choose to live in it. Others of you will choose to reject it. But no matter where you go, it will be there. The Bible says that nothing can separate us from the love of Christ.

If you are currently rejecting this love, know this: you will never be given up on. You will never do anything so horrible that Jesus' death couldn't be enough to cleanse you and connect you to God. You will also never be complete without God. We were made in His image and only when we have Him as part of us will we find what completes us.

For those of you who have experienced and accepted God's unconditional love, you are secure. What Jesus did on the cross is enough. You will have times where you feel closer and further away from the love of God. That is not because His love is changing. It is because you are. The more you spend time with Him, the more you will feel His love.

Finally, I want to tell you that the love of God is complete. God does not need us, but He did chose us. We do not need to prove our love to God. Too often we become trapped in a battle to become "good enough" for God. It can't happen. He is perfect. I missed that mark long ago. Instead of trying to prove you are good enough for Him to love you, shift your focus to celebrating who He is. He is complete. Let's focus on all of the things the Bible tells us about Him and just love Him back.

Having lived under the concrete, in the dirt, I admit many of the concepts in this chapter may be really hard. You may not know how to love. You may not know how to trust. You might be really angry still. It is okay. Remember, your life is created by the decisions you make. Let's just start with the first decision. Decide to believe in your heart and confess with your mouths that Jesus is Lord. From there, try and relax. Spend time with God and trust that if He can move planets around, create stars, and place a sun to perfectly warm the earth, He can teach you to love. He can grow you. I am very confident that he can lead you through the journey of growing in Him.

Guided Journaling Activity:

Turn to pages 114-115 and Reflect on Concepts 10-13

Chapter Thirteen: Attachments

Secure attachments can only be formed when a person is secure in themselves and their relationship with Christ. So what happens when your experience has left you insecure in yourself? In my life the answer was really obvious: My ability to attach was damaged.

Let's define attachment. By attachment, I am referring to the ability to be comfortable being yourself – the ability to approach others with a vulnerability and honesty that comes from a confidence in yourself, even your imperfections. Your interactions then become free and you have the ability to be yourself, grow your relationships, and experience life.

But I am almost 100 percent sure that my concrete and my dirt destroyed my ability to attach. How can someone who longs for dirt to consume her decaying body also be comfortable being herself? Is it realistic to think that I could approach others from a place of vulnerability and honesty, when whatever shred of confidence I might have was "set" into a concrete slab years ago?

Survivor, attachment probably feels unnatural. That skill may have been superseded by survival a long time ago. Personally, I understand survival. I know how to work hard and give everything to fight to live. Natural, healthy attachment, on the other hand, feels completely unnatural. Confidence, trust, and vulnerability...no! These are not natural to me.

I cycle through four stages in my life: (1) trust no one (2) trust a little and test people (3) give someone my full trust, and (4) realize that even my full trust is not fully trusting because of my wounds. That is it. That word: "wounds." What in the world am I expected to do with my wounds? I have a desire to fully attach, and to fully experience healthy relationships. Yet, my wounds are constantly reminding me I don't know how.

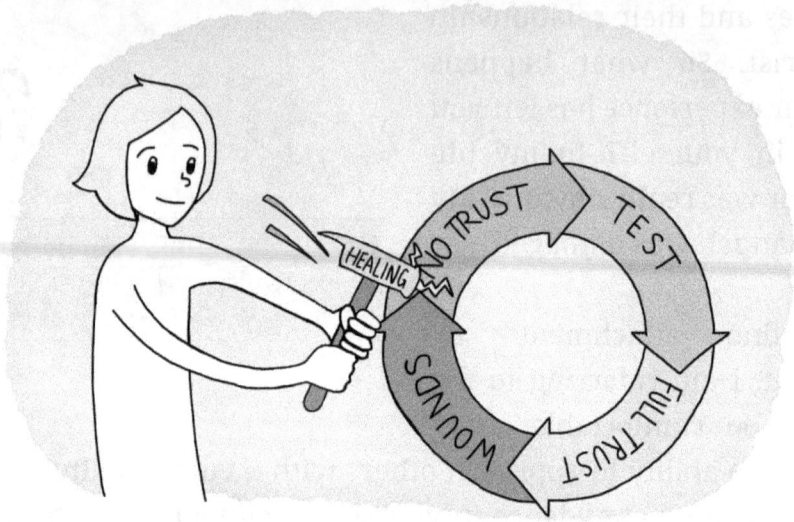

I guess that is where it starts for me. I firmly and fully believe I am made in the image of Christ. I believe there is a part of my heart, my being, and my identity that will only be complete when I allow Jesus Christ into that part of me. I feel like this need is amplified in my life because of my wounds. This need exists in you, too, regardless of your experiences in life.

Yet, my concrete tells me that I am separate, different, dirty. The chasm separating Jesus and me was enormous, and this disconnect impacted my ability to attach to Him. I honestly wasn't sure I even understood Jesus. Inside my soul, I longed to attach to Him, to let Him heal my wounds. But my behavior was the opposite. I did not trust Him. I might periodically test Him. If I "fully trusted" Him, it had to be on my terms. I recognized that my wounds were still more pervasive inside my soul, than was my ability to trust. I cycled, bounced around, and repeated these four stages over and over for years...and that made me mad. Where was Jesus, the healer? Why couldn't He just zap the open wounds in my heart and heal them? And then, He did.

The change in my life occurred instantly. It occurred when I realized this: My connection to a loving God came as a result of Jesus. Not just Jesus' death and resurrection, but Jesus' life. For Jesus' death to connect us to God, His life had to be perfect. As I began to see Jesus' life, I realized that His love could heal my wounds. They weren't healed the way I had expected. I expected my wounds to be erased, but that is not what happened. Instead the God-sized hole in my heart was filled, and because Jesus' love is so much larger than I could ever contain, that love poured throughout my body and also healed my wounded, lifeless parts. I believe Jesus' love offered me the ability to live a full, complete life. And, I am beginning to see myself through His eyes as someone created in His image.

Let's look at one story (there are many) where this occurred in Scripture. John 4 talks about a Samaritan woman who approached a well because she was thirsty. I wonder if she carried around concrete and dirt? The story tells us two things about her. First, she was a Samaritan. Jews, in that day, had no dealings with Samaritans. Could she have felt separate? Different? Second, she had five husbands and the one who she currently was with was not her husband. Could she have struggled with attachment? Could it have been that she was looking for a person to fill her wounds?

I don't know those answers, but I do know that Jesus met her and was willing to overwhelm her with love. Early in the chapter He began a conversation with her about filling her with a well of water springing up to everlasting life. He not only wanted to meet her need in that moment, but also in the future, and through everlasting life. He sought to fill her to completion.

I wonder in the back of her mind if that woman didn't understand what Jesus wanted to do. Perhaps she believed the offer wasn't for her... she had too much dirt and concrete. The reason I wonder is that Jesus lovingly assured her that He knew her. He assured her that He knew of her husbands. He recognized her wounds. But instead of accepting His love, she responded by reminding Him that she was a Samaritan. She pointed to the physical separation of their groups. He was a Jew; she was not. However, Jesus lovingly pointed her back to God and said that a day is coming when true worshipers would worship together in "Spirit and truth" (John 4:23 NIV). Jesus fully and completely reminded this woman that His love is based on God, not her actions or origins.

At this point she stated that she was indeed looking for Christ to come. Jesus assured her, again, that her need had already been met. He then told her that He is the Christ. She responded dramatically by leaving her belongings to go tell people in the city about the One who knew her.

The Samaritan woman responded to the love attachment she experienced with Jesus. I have to believe that wounded parts of her must have been healed that day. I have to believe that a confidence buried deep within her soul was found. You see, Jesus' love was greater than she could even experience. It not only filled the place in her heart that longed for the Messiah, but I believe His love must have overflowed to every part of her being. She must have been changed. She must have seen herself through Jesus' eyes.

The reason I believe this must have occurred is two-fold. First, the Bible reveals that many in the city believed in Jesus because of the woman's word that He knew her, telling her "everything I ever did" (John 4:29, NIV). The love Jesus showed this woman must have changed her so powerfully that others believed in Him also. I wonder if everything changed for her. I wonder if she went from being known as "the lady with five husbands" to having a reputation of being the woman Jesus loved so overwhelmingly that her life and her actions were completely transformed?

The second reason she must have been completely healed shows up in John 4:42. This verse says the people no longer believed in Jesus simply because of what the Samaritan woman said, but "now we have heard for ourselves, and we know that this man really is the Savior of the world" (NIV).

That verse sounds to me like she had the opportunity to point people to Jesus without emphasizing herself. She didn't seem to be hiding this overwhelming love behind her concrete or standing before others covered in dirt. She stood confidently and showing love, while pointing people directly back to the source that had taught her to love. I believe she experienced healing, attachment, love, and the ability to share all of those things with others.

Survivor, I have lived days where tomorrow seemed uncertain. Days where I simply didn't know how I could possibly fight any harder to survive. I have faced my wounds. I have looked everywhere and to everyone, except Jesus, to fill this need.

I can only tell you this. Jesus knows you. He knows the history you face. He is prepared to offer you overwhelming love. Your choice has to be to acknowledge Him. When you do, He can heal you, change you, and complete you. I think it is time – time for wounds to be healed. Time for attachment to be natural, and based on a love that is not yours. It is time for your life to look and feel different.

Guided Journaling Activity:
Turn to page 116 and Reflect on Concepts 14 and 15

Milestone 4 Guided Journaling Activity
Understanding Your Purpose

It is in the love of Christ that we are complete. As we experience His lovingkindness and His deep desire to share all of Himself with us, we learn who we are. We are His children; we are protected and safe. As His children, we grow to become like Him in the safety of that relationship.

Your fourth journaling milestone experience will challenge you to open your heart in new ways to experience the acceptance, love, and completeness Jesus offers.

Concept #1: My starting point

What do you believe about God? Who is He in your life?

_____
_____
_____
_____
_____
_____
_____
_____
_____
_____
_____
_____
_____
_____

Concept #2: My emotions

How do you feel toward God? Has your experience with abuse created any unresolved emotions toward God?

_____

_____

_____

_____

_____

_____

_____

Concept #3: My willingness

Do you believe that the love of the Father can heal you? Are you willing to be honest with Him about your feelings toward Him?

_____

_____

_____

_____

_____

_____

_____

_____

_____

Concept #4: The choice presented by free will

What emotions do you feel while processing the thought that a loving Father gave you the choice – the free will–to make good or bad decisions?

_____
_____
_____
_____
_____
_____
_____
_____
_____

Concept #5: My abuser made a choice

Are you placing the responsibility of your abuser's choice on God instead of your abuser?

_____
_____
_____
_____
_____
_____
_____
_____
_____
_____
_____

Concept #6: God is always present

How does it feel to imagine God or Jesus present when you were experiencing abuse?

_____

_____

_____

_____

_____

_____

_____

Concept #7: God wants to be part of my life

How do you feel about God wanting to be part of your life? Do you believe that He wants to do good things in your life?

_____

_____

_____

_____

_____

_____

_____

_____

_____

Concept #8: The power of God

How does your survival show that the power of God is greater than the power of evil?

_____

_____

_____

_____

_____

_____

_____

_____

Concept #9: Love and unconditional acceptance

In what ways do you see the love of God? Are there times when you have pushed away His love?

_____

_____

_____

_____

_____

_____

_____

_____

_____

Concept #10: Experiencing love

In the story in this chapter, Lizzy tested how I would respond to her desire to be close to me. She "snuck" into my bed, then began to pray that she could come to my bed, and finally verbalized how excited she was to be close to me. Lizzy was always welcome in my bed and did not need to test me to see if she would receive love. Are you testing God's love instead of accepting that it is an always available gift?

_____

_____

_____

_____

_____

_____

Concept #11: God has drawn me with His lovingkindness

What things in your life cause you to feel like God is not drawing you with His lovingkindness? Have you pushed away or ran away from this love?

_____

_____

_____

_____

_____

_____

_____

_____

_____

Concept #12: The love of Christ is complete

You are chosen, loved, and accepted. These things are found in who He is, not what you do. Who is Jesus? What can you celebrate about Him? Who is He to you?

_____

_____

_____

_____

_____

_____

Concept #13: My story is created by the choices that I make

What choice are you being asked to make in response to Christ's love? If you have not already done so, is it time for you to confess Jesus as Lord?

_____

_____

_____

_____

_____

_____

_____

_____

_____

_____

Concept #14: Encounters with Jesus will dramatically change me!

Has your relationship with Jesus resulted in dramatic life change like the woman at the well experienced? Write about your experience with Jesus.

_____

_____

_____

_____

_____

_____

_____

Concept #15: Life is found in Jesus, not me

The Samaritan woman reminded Jesus of her inadequacies. Are there areas where you push Jesus away because you feel inadequate? He wants to offer you life. How should you respond?

_____

_____

_____

_____

_____

_____

_____

_____

Milestone 5:

Embracing Your Story

Chapter Fourteen: Recognizing Roots

Abuse is not my story. My story is created by the decisions I make. I did not make the decision to be abused. What clarity! What freedom! How simple...Well, I thought it would be simple.

I sat down with pen and paper and created two columns: "My Story" and "Not My Story." But, when I was honest with myself, I had to create a third column: "I don't know."

You see, it was easy and super powerful to reject ownership of the abuse. It was easy to reject ownership of the lies I had been taught or threatened to tell. I eventually rejected the core belief that I was dirty and unwanted. But other things weren't so clear. Was my failed marriage my choice, or a consequence stemming from my inability to experience love, trust, attachment, and other fundamentals needed for a successful marriage?

Likewise, I quickly claimed that the determination I had applied to be successful in my career and sports was my choice. But I had learned that determination through my fight to survive. So, where did it fit?

As I pressed on in the battle to understand my story, the concept of roots began to emerge. You see, it really is this simple. Some very bad things have happened in my life. I have the freedom to reject those things. Likewise, I have made some really good choices in my life. I have the freedom to claim those good choices as my story. It isn't that I am negating my responsibility for bad choices, because I am not. I have made some bad choices, too, and many of those were made at times I had full power to make the right choice. I just simply didn't. I own those choices too.

Yet there is a middle category. It is fun. It is redemptive. It celebrates the fact that God can work all things together for good. It acknowledges that the bad existed but allows me to embrace the good that can come from it as God works all things together in my life – my story – for good (Rom. 8:28, NIV). Let me give you an example. Earlier I mentioned struggling to determine if my success in my career had been the result of hard work and determination stemming from survival skills learned during my abuse experience, or if success had come from my choice to be committed to my job. The answer is both. It is a root – a root firmly planted and supporting a tree.

I began my corporate career when my life was unstable. My marriage had just fallen apart. What little money I had was in envelopes and on gift cards. Being successful was not an option; it was a necessity. I applied for probably 100 jobs – and I'm not exaggerating here! I told you that I know how to fight to survive! I ended up with a couple of offers and selected one. The company chose me because my background included sales experience, and because I had completed a lengthy training program at my last job in a very short amount of time. At my new company I would begin in a mid-level sales position, rather than entry level.

The day I began, I was informed that the position I was filling had been vacated due to the previous employee's inability to perform. The position had been open for an extended period of time, and I needed to utilize my ability to learn quickly like I had done in my last job's training program. I would begin interacting with customers 24 hours later.

This was a new industry. I had no idea what they sold. I had no knowledge of how to talk about it. And, I definitely did not know how to place orders using weird DOS-based software.

Finding negative thoughts was not hard: I was stupid. I had never been smart. They would get rid of me like they had the last person. Heck, everyone got rid of me; why would it matter? I didn't matter. No one cared about me anyway. I had only had one purpose in life and it very clearly wasn't this.

Surviving was also natural to me. I knew exactly how many dollars were in my gas envelope. I didn't really have enough money for food, but I was surviving. I had to make it. I took this job. My feelings did not matter. What mattered was survival.

So the next day I smiled and talked on the phone to my first customer. There was no need to sell. She just wanted to order a UPS. Whew! I heard her say, "Order on UPS." I knew about shipping and handling providers. So, I confidently began to explain that we had many shipping and handling providers. But why was she laughing? Why were the guys sitting beside me laughing? Wonderful. Apparently in the technology world, a UPS is an uninterruptable power supply that is used to keep a server running during a power outage.

I would like to tell you that my new job became easier. It didn't. I hated every day for the first 90 days. I worked 15 or more hours per day. I took notes home to study, in what little time I had at home. I wanted to give up, but I had to survive.

At the end of 90 days, I somehow ended up ranked number one in the nation. The guys I worked with were challenged by my work ethic. I did exactly what those leading me instructed – hoping they were right – and that I would be successful. The guys saw my success, not my overwhelming lack of confidence or the absolute self-hate driving my survival mode.

My boss was a little more perceptive. She challenged me with ideas like maybe I could be successful without working 15+ hours a day, seven days a week. She tried to help me see that I was being successful. It didn't compute for me in those days. My confidence and self-concept were too low to believe that I could be responsible for something good happening to me. I still hated my job. It felt like my new master. It wasn't a person, but it felt like the next thing with control over me.

Nine months after starting my new job, I was promoted. This was so fast! It was unheard of. Six months after that, I was promoted again. After another six months, I entered into a sales coaching program. All of this time, I had been working insanely hard. I had been experiencing amazing results. I had learned to be a little happier, but still felt like a slave to my job.

When I became a coach, I finally began to realize that maybe some of my success could be attributed to me. Not everyone was willing to make the sacrifices I had made for success. Many people were smarter. Many people were better at selling. But determination was what had made me, me.

As my career has progressed, I have learned to use my determination in positive ways. I have learned that it is okay to feel pride when I do a good job. I have learned to accept kudos from others. I have learned that I have things worth sharing. I have learned that it is fun to build community as you share. I have learned that I can be both successful and happy. And, I have learned that I am in charge of my life.

There was a time when my choices were inspired by fear. I was still in the dirt with concrete weighing on my being. There is no doubt that I learned to strive for perfection and to fear demise while I was in the dirt. There is no doubt that low self-worth and fear of failure drove me to refuse to give up. BUT, there was a middle category. No, I did not choose to learn the negative drivers that defined my early career, but it was my choice to realize the things I was doing were unhealthy. I began to make intentional choices to change my lenses. I still worked really hard to be successful, but not because I had to; instead I worked hard because I chose to do so.

I chose which sacrifices I was willing to make to be successful. I chose to appreciate the benefits of my hard work. I chose to contain my work into a more manageable number of hours. I chose to develop community by sharing success with others.

In this book, I have referred to dirt as negative. I have focused on decomposition and decay, which are real attributes of dirt. But dirt has other attributes also. Dirt is the home of life-giving roots. Those roots provide stability. Those roots allow for growth.

And that is just it...Growth. We begin to really grow when we start seeing that though things may have been terrible and unfair, we are good. We have the power through Christ to acknowledge that what others intended for bad, God can use for good.

I have always wanted to help my children keep their choices and their beings as separate but connected things. I teach them to take responsibility for their choices but to remember that bad choices do not have the power to define their entire person. We will all make some bad choices, and will be sorry that we did. It can end there. We don't need to enter into cycles of making our mistakes larger than they really are. Each of us makes millions and millions of choices. No one choice has the power to define us. Many, many choices come together to be pieces of our very complex beings. These pieces come together to make a more complete view of ourselves.

We recently adopted a cute little fur ball that we call Lou Lou. She is fun and a perfect fit for our family. Lou Lou knows where she needs to potty. We take her outside upon request. Well, the other day Lou Lou did not go outside. She peed in my house! I was so mad. It is just one of those things that I hate. I immediately scolded her, "Bad dog. Bad dog. Bad Lou Lou." As I pushed her outside, my son said, "Mom, are you mad?" I said, "Yes, Lou Lou is a bad dog." David, my son, looked at me and said, "Mom, that is not true. Lou Lou is a good dog. She just made a bad choice." I apologized to him and Lou Lou as I smiled inside with the pride that my son was beginning to understand that we are worth so much more than one bad choice or even many bad choices.

I want you to know that some of the things you do will be because you learned them in dirt. Where possible, reject negative thought patterns. Do not own someone else's choices. But also, pause long enough to realize that some things, like my obsession with working hard, can be grown into roots. A negative trait can be turned into a positive trait as you learn to respect yourself.

As you are growing and redirecting life patterns, you will make mistakes. Your abusers wanted their choice to define your entire self. It probably did. But one choice today does not have that power. You will fail sometimes. You will make mistakes. You are a special, unique person, and your story is made up of your choices – lots and lots of choices. Relax! Give yourself the freedom to grow. You do not need to be perfect. You aren't. But you are growing.

I have used a root analogy a couple of times in this chapter, because roots are the beauty that comes out of hard times. I think the security of roots runs really deep. I believe that my past experience with abuse did shape who I became. Rejecting the responsibility for the abuse also shaped who I became. It gave me the freedom to let my choices create my story. Finally, I believe that God saw my struggle in the dirt. I believe that long, long before I even dreamt that He was working, He already had planned to help me use the chaos, pain, harm, and heartbreak of my life to experience a fulfilled life, a hopeful life, a life overwhelmed by love, and a life where abundant love could be shared because I am securely planted. I am proud of my life. I am never alone. I make good choices because that is who I am. I make bad choices sometimes too. I have learned to forgive myself and not expect perfection. I have learned that the plan for my life is good.

Your plan is great also! Take your paper out. Where are you today? I bet there are choices you can easily remove from your personal responsibility list. These choices weren't yours. These choices go in the "not my story" column. When they try to control your thinking, actively reject them. They are not you. I bet there are also choices that you securely know that you made. These choices go in the "my story" column. Celebrate those!

You have created a story. It is you, and it is beautiful. Finally, I bet there are choices you don't know about…were they even your choice? Or were they choices made by someone else? These choices go in the middle "I don't know" column. I love the middle column. You might not know the answer yet, but your mind has already begun the process of questioning ownership of the choice. That is how it got stuck in the middle. So, accept that it is in the middle. Ask yourself if you can redirect the behavior. Could it be like my work? Is it a great choice – like being a hard worker – but stemming from the wrong motivation? Could giving yourself the freedom to relax, to fail, or to take a new risk help you transition your choice into something positive? If you find a bad choice in the middle, could that be a hint that perhaps you are overburdening yourself with responsibility? Are there behaviors that lead to the bad choice you could begin to actively reject? Thought patterns you could change? Could small changes, small choices to take control, prevent you from continuing to make the same bad decision in the future?

You see, redemption of your past is possible. Years don't have to have been completely stolen. I once believed that my abusers had that power. I believed they stole many years. But, it isn't true. I have roots. I am strong. I am planted. I am secure. And, all of those things, plus my choices for a life of abundance, are part of me. I am unique, special, and grounded in the love of Christ – and that is more than enough for anything that life presents. I am proud of my story. I am happy to have lived my life. It hasn't always been fun, but it has helped me find myself.

Guided Journaling Activity:
Turn to pages 141-143 and Reflect on Concepts 1-4

Chapter Fifteen: Changing Perspectives

I have intentionally chosen to write this book over a long period of time. Early in life, I thought my story was on hold. I believed I had made no choices. I felt that my life had revolved around what my abusers decided for me. I did not see my story because I did not believe in myself enough to accept I had the power and the strength to make my own choices.

At the time I began to write this book, I had been in counseling for almost five years. The intentional decision to invest in my healing, and the calculated choice to grow daily, had helped me find pieces of myself. When I first started writing, I couldn't define how my past could be restored, but today I feel that that picture is clear. So, I would like to tell you my story as I see it today. My viewpoint might continue to expand as I learn more about myself; but today, here is where I believe I am.

Abuse is not my story. My story is created by the decisions I make. I did not make the decision to be abused.

Unfortunately, some people did make the decision to abuse me. The darkness and destruction of that choice is their responsibility. They have to survive the horror of their choice. For a period of time, their choice placed a shadow over my story. It is true. I did live in dirt; I did bear the weight of a concrete slab separating me from the life I wanted to live. I did suffer hopelessness and decomposition in the dirt. But my life had a much larger story than just that. My time in the dirt allowed me the opportunity to watch roots grow. It allowed me to watch seeds blossom. Nourishment for plants, trees, and grasses that exist above the dirt are found in their healthy roots.

All aspects of dirt are not bad. We see dirt as filthy, unclean. But that is not the only story dirt tells. I believe that dirt tells the story of roots. I believe it tells the story of beginnings. I believe it tells the stories of life emerging.

Today, I see myself as a tree. Some trees have root structures as deep as 20 feet. That is almost four times my height! Other roots can be wide and long. No matter the root type, the root is vital for the tree to survive.

I like to imagine that my time in the dirt caused the dirt to move. In a very different way, maybe I was moving like a tiller through the dirt, making the conditions right for the seeds to take root.

An apple tree can produce up to 920 pounds of fruit. That is exponentially more than I imagined! But the tree is strong; it is planted. Not all apple seeds are given the opportunity to produce powerful fruit. But there are three common characteristics amongst trees that do grow. First, the tree started in the dirt, as a seed. Second, it fought to be strong enough to push its way out of the dirt toward the sun. Remember that even when it emerged above the dirt the roots that had been formed in the dirt still existed. They are the tree's strength. Third, and finally, apple trees that produce fruit grow around other apple trees. They fertilize from the interaction with other trees.

My story is the same. I didn't understand that the choices I was making while in the dirt would allow me to grow and produce fruit, but that is what has happened.

I was born in dirt. In dirt I learned to fight even when I did not know what it meant to fight. I was fighting for the life I live today. In dirt, I learned that the elements could be difficult but they did not have to define me. Instead, I learned to find nourishment in the dirt for my roots. I also learned that courage, independence, faith, love, relationships, and many more things are what flow through my "tree." You see, there is strength in my roots. There is a story written on the trunk of my tree. I have beauty that is revealed in my leaves. There is power to be shared as "fruit" to nourish others.

I fought to be strong enough to dig my way out of the dirt. But, I did not fight alone. My cheerleaders, investors, and counselors fought with me. Most importantly, my heavenly Father fought with me. At times, when I could no longer fight, they even fought for me. The first part of me that emerged above the dirt was the part that refused to give up. Shortly after, a curiosity part emerged. It needed to know how to live above the dirt. And, finally, a health part emerged. This part looked at me, above the dirt and in my roots, and connected my experience to my life. It helped me realize what was and what was not my story; and it helped me celebrate who I truly am.

I am growing around other apple trees. We may not have all been planted in the same conditions. Some were gently placed by a farmer's hand and grown with intentionality and love. Others grew in conditions similar to mine. But we all grew. We all have roots. We all have trunks with stories written on them. We all find beauty in leaves. We all enjoy sharing fruit. But mostly, we all know that the conditions that keep us alive come from our heavenly Father.

I hope you never give up. I hope you can celebrate the choices you did make. I hope you can relieve yourself from the responsibility of choices that were made for you or to you. I hope you grow. I hope you are planted with others. I hope you produce fruit. I hope you can experience the love of the Father who guides and encourages your growth.

Growing is not easy. I am even pretty confident that the weight of apples on your branches might not be easy. But you don't have to be alone. As you choose to grow you will find others growing around you who will encourage you. You will provide encouragement as a cheerleader. You will give seeds as an investor to others. Your life will have impact. Your story will be created by the decisions you have made, and will continue to make.

So, let's go grow! Let's go produce. Let's remind the world of the beauty of our leaves.

Guided Journaling Activity:

Turn to page 143 and Reflect on Concept 5

Chapter Sixteen: Rest and Relax

At the end of many counseling sessions, I listen as my counselor says, "Make sure you rest. You have worked hard. You might be tired." She is right, isn't she, Survivor? Healing work is hard. Living life is hard. Being intentional with your choices is hard.

Finding time to rest is also a choice. But learning to relax during that time is a lifestyle. Let's talk about both.

Resting your body provides relief. Many scientific reviews have shown the power that rest has, and its impact on your overall health. I am currently working for an international company. Many of my employees reside in other countries. We greet one another with opposing statements of good morning and good evening. The balance of our schedule has necessitated meetings at both very late hours and very early hours. This schedule has been difficult on my body. I often find myself overly tired, trying to recover sleeping hours on the weekend, or simply disoriented as to if I should sleep or be awake. I have had to create boundaries in my schedule to ensure that my body is supplied the rest it needs to function properly.

Relaxing, on the other hand, is a lifestyle. I hope your journey through this book has reminded you that you are beautiful and that you were created for a purpose. I hope you feel the power of being uniquely you. Relaxing, I believe, is an inner calm and acceptance. It is an acceptance of yourself and recognition of the beauty around you.

I had an investor once tell me that he did not believe that I knew who I was. He reminded me that I was made uniquely, individually, and in the image of Christ. He told me my actions led him to believe that I did not understand this reality, because if I did, I wouldn't be able to be ordinary. I am created extraordinary! There is not another me in all of creation!

You are extraordinary also. You were created with purpose. You were created to live a full and abundant life.

But that is so hard when concrete is heavy. Dirt settles into cracks and can be forgotten. Living the abundant life you are given can seem impossible. Believing in yourself can often feel like a future event.

Two things in my life really helped me as I began to embrace self-acceptance and purpose. First, I gave myself permission to be enough. Second, I challenged myself to define and celebrate my life's purpose.

It is so easy to become stuck in "fixing" mode. I am in the healing process. I am making my children's lives better. I am trying to pay bills. I am competing with a long list of errands for small amounts of quality time. My life can be busy. I can quickly feel like I will never arrive. Where was I scheduled to arrive anyway? Was it the American dream? Oh yes, I need 2.5 children, a husband, a house, a great income, and the latest gadget. Or was it the misrepresented Christian blessing? You know, the one that says I am blessed because God has rewarded me financially. Or, wait, was it healing that I was pursuing? I need to learn to set boundaries, do my counseling assignments, and reject false beliefs about myself.

STOP! Your story, is created by the decisions you make. Your dreams are yours. This revelation overwhelmed my heart one day in my prayer group. I have the privilege of spending time with a phenomenal group of ladies for one hour during my Wednesday lunch. These women are passionate. Our only purpose for the hour is to pray and relax with Jesus. Vulnerability is a respected and free gift in this group.

One particular day near Thanksgiving I listened to these women as they were sharing honestly about their lives. I listened beyond their words and saw hearts seeking overwhelming love. Most of these women possessed "the American Dream"; by worldly definitions, they had everything. But they all wisely knew that there were many more important things. While listening, my heart turned inward. Each of us had such different life situations but our hearts were crying out for the same thing...we wanted to relax. In that moment God clearly told me that I was missing the overwhelming blessings that He was placing in my life because I was trying so hard to define blessings by my checklist of acceptable blessings! God's blessings for me were not found in my definition but in His creativity.

Relax, Victoria, your life is a large open field! Your choices decide what is placed in that field. You have the privilege of choosing your dream. Use your creativity, your success, and your matrix of what's important. It is your dream. You were uniquely created with a very special life purpose.

Relax, Survivor, your life is a large open field, too! Your choices decide what is placed in that field. You get to choose your dream. Use your creativity, your success, and your matrix of what's important. It is your dream. You were uniquely created with a very special life purpose.

When I remove the lenses of pre-defined success, I have the freedom to succeed in the realm of gifting that is built on my personal creativity. I embrace freedom. I remove expectation. I set paths that matter to me. I harness energy doing things that are natural to me.

Your life is not defined by others. They do not make your choices. Your life, your story is created by the choices you make.

Let's take, for example, this book. What if you don't learn proper boundaries? What if investors are too hard to find? Would these things make healing harder? Yes. But what if you found other healing paths that this book hasn't explored? What if adult coloring books grounded you in a way that made your healing journey faster? Would our paths be different? Yes. Would either you or I be right? As long as we were both making healthy decisions, we would both be right, with special and unique approaches.

Let's take a moment to reflect on where we are today. You will need four things: (1) your bank statement, (2) your schedule, (3) your phone, and (4) your emotions. Now, do this exercise four times, once with each of the things listed. Rank what that item tells you is most important. What is your money pointed toward? How are you spending your time? Who do you talk to most regularly? What does your heart tell you actually matters?

This exercise should give you some insights into yourself. The things that don't align with your heart and emotion are clutter. Remove the clutter. Beyond things required to sustain life, is there the opportunity to remove excess and be more intentional in your pursuit to live your dream? Could you find freedom to relax as you pursue things that your heart identified uniquely you?

There is a second activity that has been powerful in my life as I learned to relax and become who God created me to be. This exercise was deeply spiritual and intensely personal. I chose to pursue this exercise in a very visual way, because seeing it in a larger-than-life way allowed the concept to sink into my heart each time I glanced in its direction.

Here is what I did. I removed all decorations from my bedroom wall. My new "decorations" were five flip-chart sized post-it notes:

Paper #1 said, "God, Jesus, and the Holy Spirit are..."
Paper #2 said, "The Bible says I am..."
Paper #3 said, "My unique gifts and blessings are..."
Paper #4 said, "Lies and false beliefs from Satan that I reject are..."
Paper #5 said, "Dates and milestones where Jesus showed His love in my life are..."

These five papers were defining, powerful, and inspirational, and they taught me to recognize things I might have otherwise missed. The papers allowed me to experience the Bible in a new way. I praised directly from poster #1. I choose to believe the truths of poster #2 even if I did not yet know how to embrace the concept. I learned what I loved to do, what made me uniquely me, from poster #3. I stopped negative thought patterns that previously consumed me with poster #4. And, finally, I became overwhelmed by my purpose by recognizing Divine love with poster #5.

These two exercises set me on a direction to understand and define myself. I learned that my life could be lived by the definition of the dreams that were creatively for and were uniquely me. I released myself from the burden of succeeding or receiving blessings that someone else defined. My life is different. My passions are different. My energy explodes when I live in my passions.

I then aligned my time, my money, and my communication to my heart's desire. My emotions found peace as I invested my energy into things that aligned with who I am.

Finally, my posters remind me that I can live in wonder. There is so much good. Overflowing love exists in my world every single moment. I was made for a purpose. I am special and unique. My blessings and my gifts are so different from anyone else. I want to be me, not an American standard. I don't have to live in negativity and lies. I don't have to strive. I can stop, pause, listen, watch, and see blessings happening around me every single day. I am not alone. When I listen to lies or become so busy, I don't focus on all of the blessings around me.

As I grew in these exercises, here is what happened. I found Victoria. I found myself. I accepted myself. I learned to love myself. I released myself from being someone else. I relaxed and learned that I was enough.

Learning to relax is a lifestyle. It is a reward. It is the reward of being you. It is the reward of growing, of healing, and of trusting that you, with Christ, are enough. You can't choose to relax today. But you can decide to make the choice to learn who you were created to be. Eventually, all of the good choices you made on your healing journey plus your choice to know yourself will compile into self-acceptance and eventually, into relaxation.

What you can do today is choose to begin to know yourself. When I started the process of meeting myself, my life was a mess. My time was pointed at things that would never define me. My money was flying away because I had no plan for it. My communication with others was infrequent and did not show people they were important. My emotions were so suppressed that I did not know they existed. But I was living the dream! I was making good money, my time was focused on upward promotion, and my communication was crisp – but without any emotional connection. I looked like a successful professional to the world. But where was Victoria? Did I even exist? Was I spending appropriate time with the people I loved? It is not that any of the things I did were bad. They were simply without purpose.

Relaxation will come when you begin to live your life, your purpose, and your dreams. I know you will find it. Don't forget God. Do you remember the God-sized hole in your heart that I mentioned earlier? You need to fill it.

Rest is a little easier. It is a momentary decision. Rest is very important on your path to relaxation. Relaxing is a lifestyle. It is not dependent on the things going on around you. Rather, it is realized upon knowing you have the freedom to be uniquely you – exactly who God created you to be.

Guided Journaling Activity:

Turn to pages 144-145 and Reflect on Concepts 6, 7, and 8

Chapter Seventeen: Grow

In this last chapter, I would like permission to be your best friend, your mentor, your mom, or any other significant individual in your life. I want to stop and hug you tightly. I want you to know that I am proud.

I have watched you over the years. I have watched you seek to find your own self. I have watched you struggle to separate from a past that continually sought to engulf you. I have watched you win. I have watched you lose. But, mostly, I have watched you never give up.

I know you have always believed deep down inside of you that you had purpose. Today, the twinkle in your eye tells me that that belief has erupted into a reality you now embrace.

You have told me your healing journey was important. Your confidence today tells me that you have found your path. You seem to have a distinct understanding of the impact your choices have on your life. You are pursuing choices that fulfill your dreams.

As you continue moving forward in your story, keep growing. Learning and curiosity will always serve you well. Growing happens as many small changes accumulate into something powerful. Every little step leads you deeper into your journey. It will be wild. It might be crazy! It will be exactly the journey that brings you peace, passion, and boundless energy.

Survivor, as a new friend, I hope you have celebrated with many people. I know you have grown while working through this book. I know you have reason to celebrate! Thank you for allowing me to share part of my experiences and my story with you. I believe in you. Never quit growing. Live your life, your dreams!

Guided Journaling Activity:

Turn to page 145 and Reflect on Concept 9

Milestone 5 Guided Journaling Activity
Embracing Your Story

You are not ordinary. You were created extraordinary, in the image of Jesus Christ Himself. As you embrace your story, you will experience the freedom to be uniquely you. You will recognize blessings and experience the wonder that exists around you every day. You will relax and grow.

Your fifth journaling milestone experience invites you to embrace your story – the story of victory. It is the story of the blessing of being uniquely you.

Concept #1: Abuse is NOT my story

Create a list of experiences in your life that are not part of your story. Take time with each experience to acknowledge that although it happened, you will no longer give it the power to define your life.

_____

_____

_____

_____

_____

_____

_____

_____

_____

_____

_____

_____

Concept #2: My story is created by the decisions I make

Now, make a list of the decisions you have made, both good and bad. Recognize that these decisions are your story. How can you learn to live in the freedom that your decisions direct your story?

_____

_____

_____

_____

_____

_____

_____

_____

Concept #3: Was it my decision?

List below the things that you still don't understand. Were those things your choice or not?

_____

_____

_____

_____

_____

_____

_____

_____

_____

_____

Concept #4: Roots are the beauty that come out of hard times

How has God allowed something you learned during a hard time to be a positive quality in your life today? If you have negative choices or behaviors that still imprison you, could it be that you are stuck in these because your experience still has too much power? Could you allow Jesus to set you free?

_____

_____

_____

_____

_____

_____

_____

Concept #5: As I grow, my perspective may change

How would you tell your story today?

_____

_____

_____

_____

_____

_____

_____

_____

_____

_____

Concept #6: I am created in the image of Christ

What have you discovered about yourself that is special, beautiful, and unique?

_____

_____

_____

_____

_____

_____

_____

Concept #7: God's blessings are not found in your definitions, but in His creativity

What blessings has God given you? How do you remind yourself to accept the creative blessings God has specially planned for you and not limit Him to your definition of blessings?

_____

_____

_____

_____

_____

_____

_____

_____

_____

Concept #8: Beginning to relax

Two activities were mentioned in the chapter. Both were designed to help you embrace your heart and experience the unique you created by God. How will you use these activities to discover who God created you to be?

_____

_____

_____

_____

_____

_____

_____

_____

_____

Concept #9: Grow!

What freedom and hope have you experienced as you invested time working thorough this book on your healing journey? What growth are you celebrating today?

_____

_____

_____

_____

_____

_____

_____

_____

_____

9 780999 836013